The Old World

Exploring Human History As In The Bible

ARUL VELUSAMY

'Bible Education For Adults' Series

RABBONI LABORATORIES
TO THE GLORY OF GOD. IN SERVICE TO MAN.

Copyright Statement

Copyright © 2014, Arul Velusamy.

All rights reserved. No part of this publication may be reproduced, distributed, or transmitted in any form or by any means, including photocopying, recording, or other electronic or mechanical methods, without the prior written permission of the publisher, except in the case of brief quotations embodied in critical reviews and certain other noncommercial uses permitted by copyright law.

When requested, permission normally may be granted to Christian entities, with no commercial interest, whose sole purpose in reproducing this material is in line with the vision of 'Operation Josiah', as available in the website, http://operationjosiah.org.

For permission requests, write to the publisher, addressed "Attention: Publication Permissions", at the address below.

Rabboni Laboratories,
200, Mawney Road,
Romford - RM7 8BU.
United Kingdom.
www.rabboni-labs.com
email: info@rabboni-labs.com

Scripture taken from the New King James Version®. Copyright © 1982 by Thomas Nelson. Used by permission. All rights reserved.

ISBN: 978-0-9932945-0-1

Printed in India.

Dedication

I dedicate this work to my Lord, saviour, teacher, shepherd, brother and best friend, Jesus the Christ, who, being in the form of God, did not consider it robbery to be equal with God, but made Himself of no reputation, taking the form of a bondservant, and coming in the likeness of men and being found in appearance as a man, He humbled Himself and became obedient to the point of death, even the death of the cross [Philippians 2:6-8] to redeem a wretch like me.
Arul Velusamy.

Table Of Contents

Copyright Statement	2
Dedication	3
Table Of Contents	4
List Of Figures/Tables/Extracts	5
Preface	7
Acknowledgements	11
I. Introduction	13
II. Beginnings	15
A. Creation Week - Chronological Order	15
B. Creation - Topical Order	39
III. Pause & Consider - How Was Creation Before Man's Fall?	49
IV. Fall	51
A. Deception & Disobedience	51
B. Judgment	55
C. Life Outside The Garden	62
V. Pause & Consider - How Was Creation After Man's Fall?	65
VI. Spread Of Sin	67
A. Murder & Curse	67
B. Ungodly	71
C. Godly	73
VII. Pause & Consider - How Would The World Have Looked Like With Cain's Line And Seth's Line Inhabiting The Earth?	79
VIII. Judgment (Noahic Flood)	81
A. State Of The World	81
B. Preparation For The Flood	85
C. The Flood	89
IX. Pause & Consider - What Are The Implications Of Noahic Flood?	99
X. Glossary	101

List Of Figures/Tables/Extracts

Figure 1 - Cosmic Microwave Background Radiation In The Universe.23
Figure 2 - Taxonomic Ranks In Biology............................29
Figure/Table 3 - Kingdoms In Biology..............................30
Figure 4 - Design Of A Bacterial Flagellum........................32
Figure 5 - Different Layers Of Rocks As Seen In Grand Canyon.....33
Figure 6 - Index Fossils..37
Figure 7 - Adam and Eve Seal......................................62
Figure 8 - The Genealogy Of Adam..................................74
Figure/Extract 9 - Sumerian King List.............................78
Figure/Table 10 - The Godly And The Ungodly Lines................79
Figure 11 - The Timing Of The Flood...............................84
Figure/Table 12 - Animals And Birds In Noah's Ark................88
Figure 13 - Comparing Noah's Ark With Modern Ships...............88
Figure 14 - Noahic Flood - Timeline...............................93
Figure 15 - Gilgamesh Epic..94
Figure 16 - Atrahasis Epic..94
Figure 17 - Boat In Chinese.......................................95

Preface

The Bible is God's revealed Word.

The material presented to you is part of a series of materials prepared to enable you to get rigorous, intimate and exhaustive knowledge of the Bible. It is my earnest desire that many of you who may use this material may be equipped enough, for the Lord Jesus Christ to use you as pillars in the body of Christ (The Church).

In the beginning, God created the heavens and the earth.

The pinnacle of God's creation on earth was man, made in God's own image. God gave man free-choice, perhaps not wanting to have a programmed being at the pinnacle. God expected man to choose to stay in synchrony with God's will and relate to God in a manner consistent with relating to one's maker. Man, however, fell far short of this expectation. God, despite his love towards man, could not pretend that nothing had gone wrong, as He was not willing to compromise on quality, in the sense of holiness, righteousness, perfection etc.

It was in this context, that God embarked on a long, costly and painful journey of making provision for the restitution of man, through a legitimate route of acknowledging the problem and providing a just and a legal recourse out of it.

God's interaction with human beings during the journey of making provision for the restitution was in two levels.

On one level, God interacted with individuals in order to restore them. Some examples of such individuals would include people from before Noahic flood like Adam, Enoch etc, people from after the flood and outside of Israel like Job, Nebuchadnezzar etc and people of Israel like Moses, Samuel etc.

On another level, God interacted with people groups or nations as a whole, in order to provide them habitations and allow them to grope for him and find him. In some extreme situations like when some nations even went to an extent of sacrificing children on fire etc, God had to isolate some of these nations so that they do not corrupt other nations and had to ultimately judge them by dispossessing them of their habitation and in some cases destroying them.

During the course of this two level interaction, God also chose a few individuals, Abraham, Isaac, Jacob, David and Solomon and a nation, Israel, to provide a proper framework to bring in the provision for the

The Old World

restitution of man in the form of the Messiah (Jesus the Christ, Yēšūā' Ha Māšîa, יֵשׁוּעַ הַמָשִׁיחַ).

The Messiah, despite being sinless, shed his blood and laid down his life as a propitiation of man's sins. In the Messiah, man has redemption through the blood, the forgiveness of sins, according to the riches of God's grace. In the Messiah, in the dispensation of the fulness of times, God intends also to gather together in one, all things, both which are in heaven and which are on earth.

The Bible elaborates the above, in great detail with references to history, theology, anthropology, law, prophecy, science, geography etc. 'Bible Education for Adults' series of materials have been prepared as aids for people to get rigorous, intimate and exhaustive knowledge of these elaborate details.

The first of the materials in this series is what you are holding in your hands - 'The Old World' and this covers the first few chapters of the first book in the Bible - 'Genesis'. The Bible refers to a worldwide cataclysmic flood during the time of Noah, which is about 1650 years after the creation of man. According to the narration provided in the Bible, this flood changed the earth in some fundamental ways and hence the world before the flood could be legitimately called the 'old' world, as referred to, by apostle Peter in 2 Peter 2:5. It is the history of this 'old world' that the material in your hands currently deals with.

The material is organized into chapters, sub-chapters and sections. Chapters are indexed with capital roman numerals. For instance - 'II. Beginnings'. Sub-chapters are indexed with capital alphabets. For instance - 'A. Creation Week - Chronological Order'. Some chapters are not subdivided into sub-chapters.

Each chapter (if the chapter has no sub-chapters) or sub-chapter is presented with the following sections (indexed by small roman numerals) -
- (i) 'Bible Passage' section: The relevant Bible passages are referenced in this section so you can read and meditate on the Bible first hand, first.
- (ii) 'Summary' section: A summary of the Bible passage is presented.
- (iii) 'Entities' section: Some of the crucial entities referred to, in the Bible passage, are listed.
- (iv) 'Introductions' section: Some of the entities which are introduced

Preface

for the first time in the Bible passage and have scriptural significance are listed.

(v) 'Name of God' section: Name(s) of God revealed in the Bible passage is(are) listed and discussed.

(vi) 'Deeper Questions' section: Some deeper questions are asked and answers are discussed.

(vii) 'Explore' section: Extra Biblical ideas that are relevant to the current Bible passage are presented.

All the above sections are not necessarily presented for all chapters/subchapters. However, the roman numerals of the specific sections are retained as provided here (even if some previous sections are absent) for the sake of consistency.

Biblical references are presented in two ways. Current (the passage currently being discussed) and backward (a passage which has already been discussed) references are enclosed within '[' and ']'. All other Biblical references are enclosed within '{' and '}'.

Cross references within this material are made indicating the chapter, sub-chapter, section and serial number within the section. For instance question 5 within section (vi) of chapter II, sub-chapter A is denoted by II.A.vi.5. Cross references within the same level of content excludes reference to the same and higher levels. In other words, when a question 5 is referred to within the entities section of the same sub-chapter, the reference is denoted as vi.5 (ignoring the same and higher levels i.e. sub-chapter and chapter respectively).

For comments and feedback on the material, please quote the relevant section in the above format and write to info@rabboni-labs.com.

May God grant you all the wisdom as you endeavour to understand His scriptures more clearly.

May God's peace be with you.

In Christ,

Arul Velusamy.

"Your word is a lamp to my feet and a light to my path." - Psalm 119:105.

Acknowledgements

First and foremost, I would like to thank God our Father and our Lord Jesus Christ, who has considered even a wretch like me, as a servant, to steward His word.

Second, I would like to thank my entire family - my father, mother, brother in law, sister and two little nephews who have been a great encouragement in my ministry to the LORD. Special thanks is also due to my aunt, Dr. Jeya Jancy Selvi Ratnam.

Third, I would like to thank my family in the LORD, especially my friends Bro.Patrick Lawson, Bro.Issa Shabo, Pastor Peter Loo, Bro.Darren Lawrence, Sis.Janet, Bro.Siva Namadurai, Bro.Luka Ward, Bro.Mutombo Bukasa, Bro.Robin Eastwood & Sis.Ruth Eastwood, Bro.Len Tull, Bro.Jacob Oomen & Sis.Fiona Oomen, Sis.Hatun Tash, Pastor Elamparithi, Pastor S.Johnson & Sis.Mercy, Bro.Aaron & Sis.Santha, Bro.Franklin & Sis.Gunavathi, Sis.Jessy who have been extremely supportive in my attempt to prepare material for the 'Bible Education for Adults' series.

I
Introduction

All of known physical reality is spectacular and vast. The earth in which we inhabit appears to be, but a speck, in the entire universe. With some of the latest advances in astronomy and astrophysics, we are beginning to get to grips with the enormity of the universe that we live in. And the most curious thing is that, this universe, seems to conform to various laws of physics. Any thinking man, is inevitably led to ask questions such as - how did these things come into being? what is going to be the ultimate destiny for these things? what is the reason for the existence of these things?

When we begin thinking it is only the vastness (of the universe) that surprises us, molecular biologists make us think again. Some of the latest developments in molecular biology reveal the complexity of living beings, beginning with a single cell. A cell, which was assumed to be a simple blob in some quarters in the years past, is now understood to be a well designed complex factory with components which are engineering marvels. Again, this leads us to ask questions such as - what is life? where does it come from? how did we get the spectrum of life forms on planet earth? what is the purpose of living beings? what is the destiny of living beings?

There have been attempts made by various parties to answer some of the questions raised both in the areas of astronomy and biology.

To come to informed answers for the questions raised above, it is important for us to consider all available sources of information and evidences, appropriately weighted for their respective historical validity and qualification to deal with such profound subjects.

The book of Genesis (the first book of the Bible) has to be given the most prominent place in this endeavour - because it was written by Moses (a prophet), who was supernaturally attested through events such as - the parting of the Red Sea, the feeding of more than a million people from the heavens etc, verified by more than a million people who were led by Moses from Egypt to Israel. The supernatural acts give the qualification for Moses

The Old World

and the verification by the more than a million people, which is an integral part of the history of Israel, gives the historical validity for the Genesis account to be Mosaic (of Moses).

In the initial few chapters of Genesis [Gen 1:1-8:19], Moses gives a narration of how the universe came into being and how life came into being. This helps us understand the origin.

Moses subsequently gives the history of the world at that time and then narrates a cataclysmic universal flood, which ultimately destroyed the world during the time of Noah. This helps us have an appropriate lens with which to view and evaluate any extra Biblical artefact from before the time of this universal flood.

It is heartening to note the following

- Mosaic account as a stand alone account is logically sound and coherent
- There are more than enough extra Biblical evidences for the cataclysmic and universal Noahic flood
- When adjusted for the Noahic flood all available and credible extra Biblical artefacts fit well with the Mosaic account of the history of the world

In this material, we go through Genesis 1:1-8:19 and present the Biblical account of creation of the universe, creation of life (especially man), history of the world before Noahic flood and a description of the Noahic flood. We would also be examining alternative views which attempt to challenge the Biblical view and see the logical and/or historical flaws in them.

II
Beginnings

"When I consider Your heavens, the work of Your fingers,
The moon and the stars, which You have ordained,
What is man that You are mindful of him,
And the son of man that You visit him?"
Psalms 8:3-8:4

A. Creation Week - Chronological Order

(i) Bible Passage - Genesis 1:1-2:3

(ii) Summary

1. The beginning [Gen 1:1-1:2] & the first day [Gen 1:3-1:5]: God created the heavens and the earth. The earth was without form and void. Darkness was on the face of the deep. The Spirit of God was hovering over the face of the waters. Later, God created the light. The day began with darkness and ended with light (an evening and a morning respectively).

2. Second day [Gen 1:6-1:8]: God made a firmament in the midst of the waters and let it divide the waters which were under the firmament from the waters which were above the firmament. God called the firmament 'heaven'.

3. Third day [Gen 1:9-1:13]: God gathered the waters under the firmament into one place called Seas, so dry land (Earth) can appear. God also created the grass, the herbs and the trees.

4. Fourth day [Gen 1:14-1:18]: God made lights in the firmament of the heavens (the Sun, the Moon and the stars), to divide the day from the night, and for signs and seasons, and for days and years, and to give light on the earth.

5. Fifth day [Gen 1:20-1:23]: God created the sea creatures and the birds. God blessed the sea creatures and the birds.

6. Sixth day [Gen 1:24-1:30]: God made the beasts of the earth and everything that creeps on the earth. God made man (male and female) in His own image. God blessed man and God gave him dominion over the sea creatures, the birds and the land animals.

The Old World

God gave the man, the herbs and the trees for food. God gave the beasts of the earth, the birds of the air and to everything that creeps on the earth, in which there is life, every green herb for food.
7. Seventh day [Gen 2:1-2:3]: God ended His work and rested. God blessed the seventh day and sanctified it.

Meditation Notes
Entities
....
....
....
Questions
....
....
....
Exploration Areas
....
....
....
Cross References
....
....
....
Other Points
....
....
....

Reference Notes
(iii) Entities
Beginning, God, heavens, earth, light, firmament, seas, grass, herbs, green herbs, trees, lights, sea creatures, birds, beasts of the earth, creeping things, man.
(v) Name Of God

II. Beginnings

Elohim ('ĕlôhıym, אֱלֹהִים) - is a generic term used to refer to the Biblical God. Please see further discussion in vi.4.

(vi) Deeper Questions

(1) Why is this passage considered a chronological account of creation?

Usage of specific words/expressions like 'in the beginning' [Gen 1:1], 'first day' [Gen 1:5], 'second day' [Gen 1:8], 'third day' [Gen 1:13], 'fourth day' [Gen 1:19], 'fifth day' [Gen 1:23], 'sixth day' [Gen 1:31] and 'seventh day' [Gen 2:2] (the ordinal numbers) and that too in sorted order indicates that this passage is meant to be a chronological account. Please note that the creation account as presented in this passage happened over the first 7 days (with no gaps between the days and no time expended before the first day) of existence of time.

Every creation (including time) began at the beginning. Note that this beginning of time was also the beginning of the first day. Later in the first day, the LORD created light and finished up the first day. Subsequently he had five more days of creation and 1 day of rest.

(2) What does it mean to say 'in the beginning'?

Time began at the beginning. A reference to 'before' the beginning would be invalid as 'before' is defined in time dimension which began to exist only starting at 'the beginning'. Note however, that a reference to 'in the absence of time' would be valid. Entities which transcend time, for instance, God, by definition can exist in the absence of time and bring about the existence of entities including even time. All entities created in the creation week had a beginning, whereas God Himself transcends time and therefore did not have a beginning.

(3) Who created God?

Please note that of all the entities which are real it is only the entities which are finite in some sense require a reason of existence outside of themselves. God of the Bible is presented as infinite in all senses and therefore will not require any reason of existence outside of Himself. In other words the question who created God is invalid at least in reference to the God of the Bible.

(4) Why does God use the plural Elohim ('elohıym, אֱלֹהִים) to refer to Him?

The term translated as God in scriptures is Elohim (אֱלֹהִים), which is by nature plural (three or more). In Hebrew, nouns can be singular (indicating one number), dual (indicating two numbers like 'two hands') and plural

The Old World

(indicating three or more numbers). However, God explicitly mentions that He is 'One' (echad, אֶחָד) [Deu 6:4]. Echad is a word used to refer to a 'composite unity' (as opposed to a 'simple unity') as in the case of 'one flesh' (man and wife) [Gen 2:24]. Therefore God is to be understood as a 'composite unity' who has at least (a further study of scriptures would reveal that it is actually 'exactly' instead of 'at least') three distinct facets.

(5) Why are two different words used in the process of creation - 'create' (bara', בָּרָא) and 'make' ('aśah, עָשָׂה)?

To describe the creation process, God uses 2 separate words in Genesis 1 and 2 - create (bârâ', בָּרָא) and make ('âśâh, עָשָׂה). 'Create' normally may mean 'bring into existence out of nothing', while 'made' may mean 'fashion out of other existing things'. However, in regards to a few things, the Bible uses both the terms and at times in an 'interchangeable' way. For instance, in regards to the woman, both 'created' [Gen 1:27] and 'made' {Gen 2:22} are used.

(6) What precisely was the process of creation?

Please refer to the previous question and answer. Some entities seem to have come into existence purely through the 'creative' power of the Word of God. In this case, God spoke specific details and His speech led to entities 'showing up'. An example for this may be light. There are however some other entities where God spoke an intention to make something and then He made that entity out of already created entities. An example for this can be man.

(7) What do heavens and Heaven refer to?

There seems to be two distinctly different things (heavens [Gen 1:1] and Heaven [Gen 1:8]) which are denoted by the same Hebrew (shâmayim, שָׁמַיִם) word in scriptures. Heaven [Gen 1:8], which is a firmament [Gen 1:8], seems to refer to the expanse that we may call 'space' today as per the clarification that it is where the heavenly bodies are [Gen 1:14-1:15]. Heavens [Gen 1:1] on the other hand may refer to the vastness even beyond the heavenly bodies (and may include 'space' also).

(8) Was light created before the sun?

It is important to understand that in the creation week, light was created on day 1, whereas the sun was created on day 4. There is no scientific reason to say that we did not have light before the sun or any other star. Further, it is important to understand also that when the sun and the other stars were

II. Beginnings

created on day 4, they might have just been 'associated' with already existing light.

(9) Were the days in the creation week really 24 hours days as we know it today?

The term translated as 'day' is actually a Hebrew term 'yom' (yo m, יוֹם). 'Yom' may refer to one of 'the bright hours of the 24 hours day', 'the 24 hours' itself and 'an arbitrary period of time'. It is the context in which 'yom' is used, which will enable us to see which one of these meanings it points to. In the creation account, in Genesis 1 & 2, 'yom' is used in all 3 senses. In the first part of Genesis 1:5, God called the light 'yom'. This is an obvious reference to the bright hours of the 24 hours day. In the second part of Genesis 1:5, the evening and morning together are called 'yom' - an obvious reference to the 24 hours 'day' and not an arbitrary length of time (please note that the usage of the term 'first' as a qualifier for this 'yom' makes this point even clearer). The same explanation can be given for 'the second yom' [Gen 1:8], 'the third yom' [Gen 1:13], 'the fourth yom' [Gen 1:19], 'the fifth yom' [Gen 1:23], 'the sixth yom' [Gen 1:31] and 'the seventh yom' [Gen 2:2]. The 'yom' in Genesis 2:4 is an instance of an arbitrary length of time.

(10) 'The evening and the morning' - really? Shouldn't it have been 'the morning and the evening'?

Please note that the days in the creation week began with an evening and ended with a morning. This is not surprising if you note that the first day had a portion before the creation of the light (evening) preceding the portion after the creation of the light (morning). It is therefore also not surprising that according to Jewish tradition, a day begins at sunset and goes up to the next sunset.

(11) When could the light from the stars have reached the earth?

Light was created before the stars. It seems like when the stars (including the Sun) and moon were created they were just associated with the already existing light [Gen 1:14-1:16]. Given this, it is not inconceivable that light 'associated' with some or all of the stars could have been made available on the earth on the same day as the creation of the stars.

(12) Was there only one sea?

It is said that the waters under the heavens were gathered into one place [Gen 1:9]. This may imply that somehow all waterbodies were connected.

The Old World

Please note that a cataclysmic flood during the time of Noah {Gen 7} might have had a drastic effect on the earth to an extent the features of the earth today might not be representative of what was there before the flood.

(13) Does the creation account sit well with Darwinian evolution?

Careful observation of the details of both Darwinian evolution and the creation account will help us understand that both of them can not sit comfortably with each other. For instance, Darwinian evolution is a process of gradual change, whereas all of the original creation happened in 6 days. In regards to the order of appearance, land animals came before birds according to Darwinian evolution theory. According to the creation account, birds came before land animals. Needless to say that creation happened through specific and discrete 'interventions' of God, as opposed to the naturalistic evolution proposed by Darwin.

(14) Does the creation account sit well with the traditional Big Bang model?

The traditional Big Bang model proposes that something came from nothing, which is logically invalid. Further, it goes on to say that the Sun came before the earth. The Biblical creation narrative on the other hand suggests that it was a transcendent infinite being who brought time and space into existence. This is a logically coherent claim. Further, it goes on to claim that the earth was there before the Sun. These comments mean that the traditional Big Bang model does not sit well with the creation narrative.

(15) Man was created in the image and likeness of God. What does God mean when He says 'in the image and likeness' of Him?

There is one more place where a similar description is used. That is in reference to Seth, son of Adam [Gen 5:2]. Adam begot a son in his own likeness after his image and named him Seth. Adam had at least 2 sons before this - Cain and Abel. However, a similar description was not used in reference to both of them. This indicates that Seth had something which was similar to Adam which Cain and Abel had not. This is most likely the 'countenance' of Seth. If this is true, what it means is that Adam was made to look just like God.

(16) Is man special?

Man is special in multiple ways. Firstly, he was created in the image of God, unlike any other created beings. Secondly, he was given the dominion over the fish, birds and land animals.

II. Beginnings

(17) What kind of food was given to man?
Man was permitted to have vegetarian food. In specific he was allowed to have every herb that yields seed and every tree whose fruit yields seed [Gen 1:29]. Unlike this, to land animals and birds, only every green herb was given as food [Gen 1:30].

(18) Was there 'death' in creation?
Please note that the narrative indicates that there was no death in creation during the creation week.

(19) God rested on the seventh day. Why? Was He tired?
It is often misunderstood that only when people are tired they rest. People can rest even if they are not tired if they have the opportunity to do so. There is no indication in scriptures that God rested because He was tired. In contrast His decision to rest seems to be a calm and considered decision with a view of perhaps enjoying all of creation.

(20) Why did God say 'it was good' at multiple points during the creation week?
Scriptures point out that God, at multiple points suggested that 'it was good' referring to some portion or all of creation until then. For instance in Genesis 1:4. These explicit comments that God made, if not anything, at least points out that God was open to evaluate His actions and was willing to make sure they were good. This points to the humility of God. However, given His infinite wisdom, it is not surprising that what He created ended up being good even in careful second evaluation.

(21) How does God's taxonomy of life work?
All of what we may call as plant kingdom are referred to as grass, herbs that yield seed and fruit trees that yield seeds [Gen 1:11-1:12]. While this may be difficult for us to first get to terms with, we need to understand that taxonomy is a virtual classification and therefore is not pre-defined to be in one specific way universally. A similar point can be made in reference to all flying beings being referred to as birds [Gen 1:20] or all land animals being categorised as one of cattle, creeping things and beasts of the earth [Gen 1:24].

The Old World

(vii) Explore

(1) What do we call as the universe? What is a multiverse?

The universe is the totality of existence. To clarify, this term is used by theists and atheists alike and therefore the implicit assumption involved is that, the universe does not include God as part of it. Through various means and methods, we have so far observed various portions of the universe and have some idea about the universe. The universe is understood to have various planets, stars, galaxies, intergalactic space, subatomic particles and rest of matter and energy. There are some observable phenomena in the universe like microwave background radiation, redshifts corresponding to various galaxies etc. There are also some predicted parameters like the shape, dimensions, mass, volume, density, temperature for the universe. Even though we know certain things about the universe, we must be careful to observe that we haven't even scratched the surface in terms of what is there to be known.

Multiverse is the hypothetical state of infinite or finite universes that together encompasses the totality of existence. As far as observational evidence goes, there is no reason to believe in a multiverse currently.

(2) What are some known facts about the universe?

There are some things that we observe in the universe currently through scientific experiments. These observations are common input to theists and atheists alike. In these scientific observations there is no 100% guarantee that our conclusions are correct, but it would seem like the results that we have currently are sensible within our current reason. Some of these things are listed below.

(a) Cosmic Microwave Background Radiation:

In 1964, American radio astronomers Arno Penzias and Robert Wilson discovered CMB as a culmination of work initiated in the 1940s, and earned the 1978 Nobel Prize.

II. Beginnings

Figure 1 - Cosmic Microwave Background Radiation in the Universe

"Ilc 9yr moll4096" by NASA / WMAP Science Team - http://map.gsfc.nasa.gov/media/121238/ilc_9yr_moll4096.png. *Licensed under Public Domain via Wikimedia Commons* - http://commons.wikimedia.org/wiki/File:Ilc_9yr_moll4096.png#/media/File:Ilc_9yr_moll4096.png

(b) Expanding Universe:

The observation of systematic redshifts from galaxies reveal to us that the universe is expanding. Through the work of scientists including Edwin Hubble it has been established that galaxies are receding from the earth at a velocity which is proportional to their distance from the earth.

(c) Uniform Temperature:

There is uniform temperature observed in the universe at great distance.

(d) Galaxies:

There are approximately 170 billion (1.7×10^{11}) galaxies in the observable universe. A galaxy is a gravitationally bound system of stars, stellar remnants, interstellar gas and dust, and dark matter.

(e) Black Holes:

A black hole is a mathematically defined region of spacetime exhibiting such a strong gravitational pull that no particle or electromagnetic radiation can escape from it.

The Old World

(3) How old is the universe?
God has clearly communicated the age of the universe to man. In the initial part of the first day, He made the heavens and the earth [Gen 1:1, Gen 1:5]. On the fourth day He made the 'lights' in the heavens [Gen 1:14-1:19]. On the sixth day Adam was made [Gen 1:26-1:28]. The genealogy of Adam right through to Jesus is available by putting together details from various portions of scriptures {Gen 5, Gen 7:11, Gen 11, Gen 21:5, Gen 25:26, Gen 47:9, Ex 12:40, 1 Kings 6:1 etc}. Taking all these into account the first day of creation is less than about 10,000 years ago. The basis to accept Bible's account of the age of the universe is that the writers of the Bible have the qualification of being agents of a supernatural God, testified through signs and wonders and verified by the nation of Israel all through its history.

In contrast to this, in pure naturalistic models, the age of the universe is estimated based on assumptions that are unverifiable. For instance, we do observe that galaxies are receding from the earth today at a rate which is proportional to their distances from the earth. This is verifiable because this is happening even now. What is not verifiable though is, if this can be extrapolated back in time, until all the galaxies came out from a singularity (single, small point of spatial existence). However, this unverifiable idea is precisely the one used in a popular cosmological model called Big Bang to estimate the age of the universe to be about 14 Billion years. The assumption of being able to extrapolate back in time, up to a singularity, is not alone unverifiable, but also based on a predisposition to reject God's existence.

(4) What are some of the models which try to explain the existence of the universe in the present form (cosmological models)?
There are multiple competing models presented to explain the existence of the universe. Some representative sample of these are presented here:

(a) Bible (Creationism):
God created the universe. In this process of creation, He employed purely the power of His spoken word to bring into existence some things (For instance, He said 'let there be light' and light came into being) and made some things from some other created things (For instance, He took the dust of the earth and made man out of it).

The universe and all that is in it were created in 6 literal days (as we know days today) of a single week.

The heavens and the earth were created at the beginning of day 1, less than about 10,000 years ago [Gen 1:1]. Light was created later on, on day 1, even before any stellar body existed [Gen 1:3]. On day 2, some sort of expanse was created [Gen 1:6-1:7]. The stellar bodies were created on day 4 and placed in the expanse created on day 2 [Gen 1:14-1:19].

At some stage in time, God had stretched out the heavens {Job 9:8, Psalms 104:2, Isaiah 40:22, 42:5, 44:24, 45:12, 48:13, 51:13, Jeremiah 10:12, Jeremiah 51:15, Zechariah 12:1}.

(b) Big Bang (Naturalism):

The essential idea here is that the receding galaxies of today have always been receding beginning from the time when they had expanded out of what is called a singularity.

(c) Day-Age (Creationism):

This is advanced by some Christians by opting for an incorrect reading of the Genesis creation week account (Please refer to discussion in vi.9). The basic idea here is that the term 'day' in Genesis 1 may possibly mean an 'age' of perhaps even millions of years. This theory is mainly advanced to make the Bible appear as if it is consistent with naturalistic estimates of the age of the universe.

(d) Gap (Creationism):

This is similar to Day-Age theory in its attempt to use the Bible to present an universe older than 10,000 years by assuming presence of millions of years between each day of Genesis 1. This is advanced by some Christians, based on an incorrect reading of Genesis (Please refer to discussion in vi.1), to make the Bible appear as it if is consistent with naturalistic estimates of the age of the universe.

(e) Multiverse (Naturalism):

The multiverse (or meta-universe) is the hypothetical set of infinite or finite possible universes (including the Universe we consistently experience) that together comprise everything that exists: the entirety of space, time, matter, and energy as well as the physical laws and constants that describe them.

(f) Steady State (Naturalism):

According to the steady state theory, new matter is continuously created as

The Old World

the Universe expands, thus adhering to the perfect cosmological principle (the principle that the observable universe is basically the same in any time as well as any place). This is now an almost obsolete theory, when Big Bang theory gained prominence as the preferred naturalistic cosmological model.

(5) How do the different models which try to explain the existence of the universe compare?

The various models that have been advanced to explain the existence of universe can be compared along different parameters, for us to come to informed judgments of them.

For this comparison, Day-Age creationism and the Gap creationism can not be considered, because a proper reading of the Bible would tell us that these are inaccurate accounts and we can not really consider these ideas as Biblical ideas.

(a) Philosophical Validity:

In terms of philosophical validity, Biblical creation model is the only one which will qualify to be considered as a valid model.

The Biblical creation model is philosophically sound. According to this model, the totality of existence (apart from God) had a beginning. In this case, the reason for existence of the universe must be outside of this totality of existence. Also, whatever the reason was, it must be an entity which is able to conceptualise things (i.e. both reason and sentience) to bring the universe into existence. On top of all these things, this entity should be outside of time (eternal) and space (because time and space are part of universe) and should have the potency to create the things that have been conceptualised and bring them into existence out of nothing (omnipotence). God of the Bible, as per revelation, is outside of space and time, is omnipotent, has reason and sentience. Therefore, the Biblical creation model is a logically sound model.

God is infinite (unlike the entire universe or any part of it) and therefore doesn't need a reason for existence outside of Himself.

Moreover, this God revealed Himself on the face of the earth in human history, through signs and wonders which were verified by multiple people, over a period of time.

All the above points can be emphatically used to explain profound philosophical questions such as 'how can something (some finite thing)

II. Beginnings

come from nothing?' in a philosophically sound manner.

In contrast, the naturalistic models are not logically sound. For instance, the popular naturalistic model, Big Bang, claims the universe to be one which had a beginning, and that the universe is currently expanding, and once had an inflationary phase. The inevitable question in this case is if universe is all there is and if this is what had a beginning, what is the reason for the existence of the universe? Whatever the reason is, it is outside space-time and matter and therefore is not 'naturalistic' in the Big Bang sense and therefore would defeat the entire idea of a 'naturalistic' model.

Similarly other so called 'naturalistic' models can also be proven to be not naturalistic as they inevitably end up going beyond 'naturalistic' properties.

(b) Historical Validity:

In terms of observational data, Biblical creation model is the only one which will qualify to be considered a valid model. God has intervened in human history to reveal His ability as creator. He was able to perform supernatural acts involving the universe that could be verified by many people including - sending a flood to destroy all the world at a time of His choosing {Gen 7:10-8:19}, splitting the Red Sea {Exodus 15}, sun and the moon standing still {Joshua 10:1-10:13}, raising dead people back to life {2 Kings 4:8-4:37}, sending fire from heaven {2 kings 1:2-1:17} etc - which we could use to determine that He very well could have done what He claims He did, which is bringing the universe into existence in 7 days.

In contrast to this, rejecting a supernatural cause and suggesting a naturalistic cause for the existence of the universe does not have any historical merit. For instance, there is no known property of a known entity in the universe, apart from God, which can bring about the beginning of the universe.

(c) Explanatory Power:

To answer some of the questions like - 'how is the universe very fine tuned, in particular the earth, so that it facilitates life?' and 'why is there life only on earth?', the Biblical creation model has tremendous potential. In contrast, any naturalistic model miserably fails to explain these.

(d) Unanswered Questions:

There are multiple questions, concerning the universe, and new ones are being asked all the time. All of the above models have unanswered ques tions. However, unanswered questions do not necessarily mean unanswerable questions.

For instance, on the Biblical creation model, one of the questions that are being explored is 'how can we see a star which is more than 10,000 light years away if light from the star did not have the time necessary to reach us?' ('distant starlight problem').

The distant starlight problem could be rephrased as 'we just do not have enough time in the model to justify certain present day observations only through known present day attributes'.

Two things must be observed here:

- The challenge of us 'not having enough time in the model' is not alone a challenge for the Biblical model but also for the naturalistic Big Bang model
- There are various suggested answers to the challenge of not having enough time. More research is being carried out in these areas

(e) Conclusion:

- God of the Bible, based on the details of who He is, is a perfect candidate to logically explain the existence of the universe.
- God of the Bible explicitly claims Himself being the reason of existence of the universe and He attests these claims through supernatural interventions (signs and wonders) in human history.
- Atheistic, naturalistic models fall short woefully in the attempts to explain the universe
- The other theistic models also have all sorts of issues.

Based on all the above points, it is sensible to come to the conclusion that the universe came into being through the God of the Bible.

(6) What are some known facts concerning life on planet earth?

(a) Variety:

We observe a variety of life on planet earth ranging from single cell life to multicellular life, life that depends on oxygen and life that does not depend on oxygen, life that reproduces sexually and life that does not reproduce sexually etc. The variety of life forms are artificially classified into different groups at multiple levels based on shared traits (Please refer to figure 2). These levels begin at the broad level called 'domain' and then end up in the narrow level called 'species'. There are estimated to be 2+ million

II. Beginnings

species of life on planet earth.

Figure 2 - Taxonomic Ranks In Biology

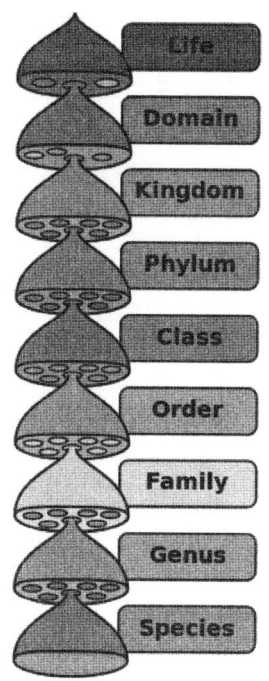

Life
Domain
Kingdom
Phylum
Class
Order
Family
Genus
Species

Courtesy: Wikipedia

The classification system, even though is reasonably useful, has a level of arbitrariness and subjectiveness to it. Please refer to figure 3 to see how different taxonomists differ on the 'kingdom' level.

Figure/Table 3 - Kingdoms In Biology

Linnaeus 1735	Haeckel 1866	Chatton 1925	Copeland 1938	Whittaker 1969	Woeseet al. 1990	Cavalier-Smith 1998
2 Kingdoms	2 Kingdoms	2 Empires	4 Kingdoms	5 Kingdoms	3 Domains	6 Kingdoms
(not treated)	Protista	Prokaryota	Monera	Monera	Bacteria	Bacteria
					Archaea	
		Eukaryota	Protista	Protista	Eucarya	Protozoa
Vegetabilia	Plantae		Plantae	Plantae		Plantae
				Fungi		Fungi
Animalia	Animalia		Animalia	Animalia		Animalia

II. Beginnings

(b) DNA:

Deoxyribonucleic acid (DNA) is a molecule that encodes the genetic instructions used in the development and functioning of all known living organisms and many viruses.

(c) Reproduction:

Reproduction (or procreation) is the biological process by which new individual organisms – 'offspring' – are produced from their 'parents'. Reproduction is a fundamental feature of all known life; each individual organism exists as the result of reproduction. There are two forms of reproduction: sexual and asexual.

(d) Objective Boundary:

In regards to generating other life through sexual reproduction, there exists an objective boundary in two levels.

On the first level, two instances of life are grouped as one 'kind' if either they can interbreed between them or they can interbreed (at least in theory) with a shared third instance of life. Once the first level boundary is resolved, one can broadly divide the instances of the same 'kind' into two 'sexes' based on their ability to interbreed.

When such an interbreeding happens, the resulting offspring is of the same 'kind'. There has never been observed a 'kind' leading to another 'kind' through reproduction.

In practice the only problem with this objective boundary is, it is hard to establish. If two instances do not interbreed it does not necessarily mean that they can not interbreed.

The taxonomic rank 'species' was supposed to represent these 'kinds'. In reality, however, what were subjectively grouped as 2 separate species, were in different cases found to be able to interbreed.

(e) Similarities Across Kinds:

Across different 'kinds' there are similarities in one or more levels - in their genetic content, possession of similar functioning organs, some features in the external appearance etc.

(f) Dissimilarities Across Kinds / Punctuations:

Dissimilarities across similar kinds along many features are marked, and can not be explained by a naturalistic, gradual change over time.

(g) Dissimilarities Within Kinds:
Within the same kind, there is wide variety in terms of features. By 2013, researchers led by David Lordkipanidze, director of the Georgian National Museum excavating in Dmanisi, Georgia found five early human skulls belonging to the same species in the same site about 62 miles from the capital Tbilisi, along with stone tools that hint at butchery and the bones of big, saber-toothed cats. The skulls vary so much in appearance that under other circumstances, they might have been considered different species, according to the study by David and Christoph Zollikofer of the University of Zurich published in the journal Science.

(h) Complex Design:

Figure 4 - Design Of A Bacterial Flagellum

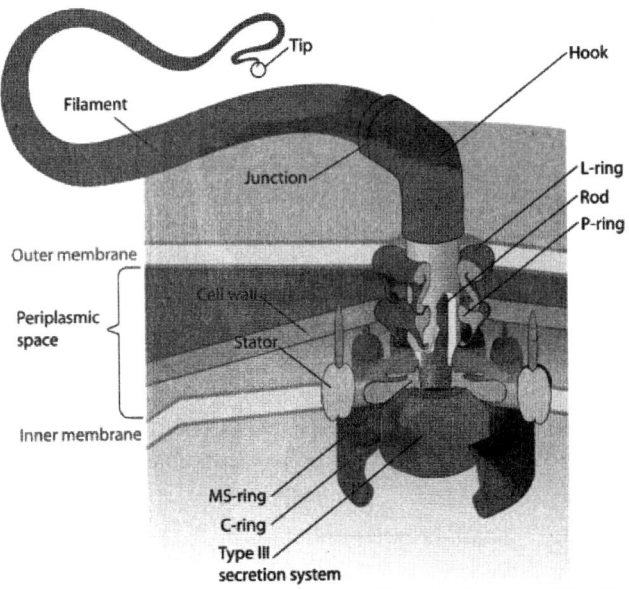

"Flagellum base diagram en" by LadyofHats - self-madeReferences: [1],[2], [3] (main 3), [4], [5] (propeller rotation), PMID 17142059 (bend).. Licensed under Public Domain via Wikimedia Commons - http://commons.wikimedia.org/wiki/File:Flagellum_base_diagram_en.svg#/media/File:Flagellum_base_diagram_en.svg

II. Beginnings

Various researches have revealed that even the simplest of life forms is not really simple in its design. They are complex and also in many cases 'irreducibly complex' (Irreducible complexity is the idea that some biological systems are too complex to have evolved from simpler or 'less complete' predecessors). Figure 4 shows the complexity of design of a flagellum of a single celled bacterium.

(i) Fossils:

Fossils are preserved remains or traces of animals, plants, and other organisms from the past, across the world. There are millions of such fossils of different species. Broadly, fossils corresponding to different species seem to appear in a specific order (even across different regions) in the different layers of rocks, indicating that there was a reasonably specific order in which different species were fossilised. It is important to note that there are notable out of order appearances and fossils of the same entity showing up across multiple layers of sedimentary rocks.

Figure 5 - Different Layers Of Rocks As Seen In Grand Canyon

Grand Canyon NP-Arizona-USA" by Tobias Alt - Own work. Licensed under GFDL via Wikimedia Commons - http://commons.wikimedia.org/wiki/File:Grand_Canyon_NP-Arizona-USA.jpg#/media/File:Grand_Canyon_NP-Arizona-USA.jpg

TOW - 3

The Old World

(7) How old is life on planet earth?
God has clearly communicated the age of life on planet earth. He created plants on the third day of the life of the universe [Gen 1:11-1:12]. On the fifth day He created birds and sea creatures [Gen 1:20-1:21] and on the sixth day land animals [Gen 1:24-1:25] and man [Gen 1:26]. The genealogy of Adam right through to Jesus is available by putting together details from various portions of scriptures {Gen 5, Gen 7:11, Gen 11, Gen 21:5, Gen 25:26, Gen 47:9, Ex 12:40, 1 Kings 6:1 etc}. Taking all these into account, the first day of life on earth is less than about 10,000 years ago. The basis to accept Bible's account of the age of life forms, is that the writers of the Bible have the qualification of being agents of a supernatural God, testified through signs and wonders, and verified by the nation of Israel all through its history.

In contrast to this, in pure naturalistic models, the age of the life on planet earth is estimated based on assumptions that are unverifiable. A crucial underlying assumption which show up in multiple ways in a naturalistic model is 'uniformitarianism'. Uniformitarianism is the speculative idea that the same natural laws and processes that operate in the universe now have always operated in the universe in the past and apply everywhere in the universe. This is a highly speculative idea with no independent observation based evidence to back it up. More crucially, it does not accommodate cataclysmic (especially worldwide cataclysmic) events, despite all available independent evidences pointing towards the existence of at least one such worldwide cataclysmic event. Please refer to discussion in chapter VIII for details of such evidences. Based on such flaky assumptions, which are against historical evidence, the first primitive life forms are estimated to be about 4000 million years, a rich variety of life to be about 530 million years and man-like hominids to be about 2 million years old.

(8) What are some models which try to explain the variety of life on planet earth?
(a) Bible (Creationism):
God created plants [Gen 1:11-1:12], sea creatures and birds of different kinds [Gen 1:20-1:21] through His spoken word. God made land animals [Gen 1:24-1:25]. God ultimately made man in His own image [Gen 1:26]. All these happened within the last 10,000 years.

II. Beginnings

All the life that God had created were created according to their 'kinds' and were intended to produce only their own 'kinds' through either sexual or asexual reproduction.

The Biblical creation model allows for a 'kind' to become different 'species' with natural selection in play, but it does not allow for a 'kind' to become another 'kind'.

(b) Darwinian Evolution (Naturalism):

Darwinism is a theory of biological evolution developed by Charles Darwin and others, stating that all species of organisms arise and develop through the natural selection of small, inherited variations that increase the individual's ability to compete, survive, and reproduce. It attempts to explain the variety of life with all different sophisticated functions developed like reproduction, circulation, digestion etc beginning from primitive single cellular life based on 'natural selection' and 'mutation' with changes happening 'gradually' over millions of years. Under this model it is assumed that no cataclysmic world-wide event happened - an idea called 'uniformitarianism'. Darwinism has nothing to say about the origin of the primitive life itself.

(c) Theistic Evolution (Theistic-Naturalism):

This is advanced by some Christians to make the Bible appear as if it is consistent with the popular naturalistic Darwinism. This is advanced by completely ignoring the creation narrative in Genesis 1 by taking that just as some sort of poetic account with no historical merit. It is then replaced with naturalistic Darwinism.

(d) Progressive Creation (Creationism):

This is advanced by some Christians by opting for an incorrect reading of the Genesis 1 account (Please refer to discussion in vi.1 and vi.9) to make the Bible appear as if it is consistent with naturalistic estimates of the age of the universe. The basic idea here is that creation happened like how it is described in the Bible except with the term 'day' meaning possibly an 'age' of perhaps even millions of years or that there was presence of millions of years between each day of Genesis 1.

(9) How do the different models which try to explain the existence of the variety of life compare?

Here we'll be comparing only the Biblical creationism model and Darwinian evolution model, as the other 2 models are misrepresentations of the

The Old World

Biblical model.

(a) Philosophical Validity:

Deoxyribonucleic acid (DNA) is a molecule that encodes the genetic instructions used in the development and functioning of all known living organisms and many viruses. DNA is information. Information is nothing without a language and language is nothing without information. In other words, we enter into a situation where we need both the language and the information developed simultaneously. In this regard, the Biblical creation model is philosophically valid in the sense that God who is outside of creation as an 'independent' cause can legitimately design both the language (the system to interpret DNA) and the information (DNA) simultaneously. In contrast, the naturalistic Darwinian evolution has no explanation for how and why the language and the information can simultaneously originate.

More broadly, the question for which different models should give a philosophically valid answer is - 'how can life come from non-life?'. Here again, Biblical creationist model provides a logically coherent answer, but a naturalistic Darwinian evolution model fails to provide any such answer.

(b) Historical Validity

In terms of observational data, Biblical creation model is the only one which will qualify to be considered a valid model. God has intervened in human history to reveal His ability as creator. He was able to perform supernatural acts involving life that could be verified by many people, including - raising up the dead {John 11:38-11:44, 2 Kings 4:8-4:37}, cleansing the lepers {Matthew 8:1-8:3}, healing the blind {John 9:1-9:7} etc - which we could use to determine that He very well could have done what He claims He did, which is create life as presented in Genesis 1.

In contrast to this, rejecting a supernatural cause and suggesting a naturalistic cause for the existence of variety of life does not have any historical merit. For instance, there is no known evidence for any kind of mutation producing a new 'kind' of life from existing life and more crucially there is no known evidence for a way in which life can come from non-life in a naturalistic way.

The presence of fossil records in a reasonably specific order is normally cited as a proof for Darwinian evolution over several million years. Accordingly, the fossils belonging to different layers in the rocks are

II. Beginnings

dated to different periods of history which evolutionists call as Paleozoic, Mesozoic, Cenozoic periods and some of the predominant fossils (called index fossils) are even used to date rock layers in different parts of the world.

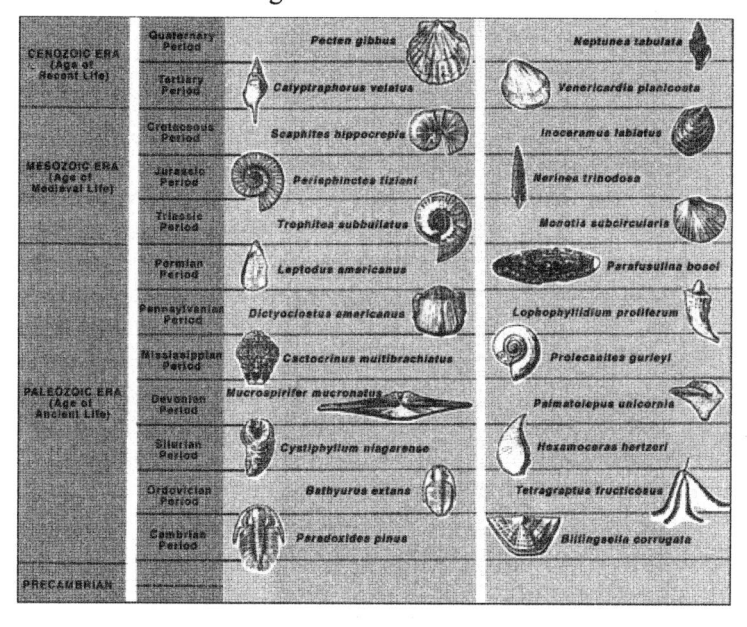

Figure 6 - Index Fossils

"Index fossils" by United States Geological Survey - http://pubs.usgs.gov/gip/geotime/fossils.html. *Licensed under Public Domain via Wikimedia Commons* - http://commons.wikimedia.org/wiki/File:Index_fossils.gif#/media/File:Index_fossils.g if

However, a closer look at the details of the fossil record would help us understand that using fossil records that show up in a rough order, as a proof for Darwinian evolution over millions of years is problematic for the following reasons:

- Precommitment to gradual changes alone: Evolutionists assume the fossil records have formed only due to gradual accumulation of sediments and therefore each layer is laid over millions of years. This is clearly an assumption with no evidence to backup. In contrast, there exists plenty of archaeological artefacts that point to the fact that all the ancient civilizations had observed a worldwide catastrophic flood (Please refer to VIII.C.vii.1 for more details).

- Marine fossils high above sea level: Dr.Andrew Snelling in his article 'What are some of the best flood evidences' written on Feb 13 2015 notes that Kaibab limestone in Grand Canyon has marine fossils about 7,000 - 8,000 feet above the sea level. These fossils could not have been formed without a catastrophic event taking marine beings high above their current abode and depositing them on high rocks.

- Multilayer fossils: It has been observed many times that some fossils cut-through multiple layers of rocks. This is a clear evidence of these fossils being deposited as a result of at least one catastrophic event, as in this case, clearly, the many different rock layers have formed in rapid succession (say, multiple layers laid out within a day) to preserve the entire organism across different layers of assumulation of sediment.

- Living fossils: It is observed that species like coelacanths, which should have been extinct about 65 million years ago, according to the evolutionist assumptions, because they do not show up in some of the higher rock levels, actually are alive even today. This is to say that if a species shows up as fossils only in a certain rock level and not later, there is no reason to think the former species was removed through natural selection.

From the above observations, it must be understood that fossil records over several rock layers are not necessarily to be taken as fossils deposited over millions of years i.e. proof for Darwinian evolution. In contrast, there is every evidence to suggest that a cataclysmic worldwide event, seems to be very true. In other words, 'uniformitarianism' seems like a baseless (unscientific) precommitment.

(c) Explanatory Power

Observations of various species in the fossil records and various living species help us note that there is no way of organising species in a specific way where you can note a seamless transition from features in one species with the features in another species. In other words, 'complex', 'well formed' features seem to abruptly show up in different species. This is simply not scientifically justifiable in Darwinian evolution.

II. Beginnings

The Biblical creation model on the other hand is high degree of explanatory power. God who is outside of creation, who is sentient, is capable of conceptualising designs of organs/systems/features and bringing them into existence through his omnipotence.

(d) Unanswered Questions

In the Biblical creation model, there is currently multiple attempts to establish how the fossils show up in roughly specific order. It must be carefully observed that the fossils showing up in such an order is permitted in this model and it therefore not a evidence to disprove this model.

(9) Further References:

For further details on some of the areas which we have just touched upon, please look out for research material made available by various ministries which have been established to study 'creation', such as the following.

- Creation Ministries International - http://creation.com/
- Answers in Genesis - https://answersingenesis.org/
- Christian Apologetics and Research Ministry - https://carm.org

B. Creation - Topical Order

(i) Bible Passage - Genesis 2:4-2:25, 1 Chronicles 1:1

(ii) Summary

1. Context [Gen 2:4-2:6]: The narrative in the passage corresponds to the history of the heavens and the earth when they were created. More specifically it begins at the time where there was no plant or herb of the field yet as the LORD God had not caused it to rain and there was no man to till the ground. At this time the LORD God had made a mist go up from the earth to water the whole face of the ground.
2. Man [Gen 2:7, 1 Ch 1:1]: The LORD God formed man of the dust of the ground and breathed into his nostrils the breath of life and man became a living being.
3. Provisions [Gen 2:8-2:15]: The LORD God planted a garden eastward in Eden. In the garden, the LORD God made every tree grow that was pleasant to the sight and good for food. The tree of life and the tree of knowledge of good and evil were also in the garden. There was also a river which went out of Eden to water the

The Old World

garden and from there it parted to become four river heads - Pishon which encompasses Havilah where there is good gold, Bdellium and Onyx stones, Gihon which encompasses Cush, Hiddekel/Tigris which goes toward the east of Assyria, and Euphrates. The LORD God put the man in the garden to tend and keep it.

4. Commandment [Gen 2:16-2:17]: The LORD God commanded the man that he may eat from every tree freely but shall not eat of the tree of the knowledge of good and evil, for in the day that he shall eat of it he shall surely die.
5. Companion [Gen 2:18-2:24]: The LORD God realised it was not good for man to be alone and decided to create a helper comparable to man. The LORD God formed every beast of the field and every bird of the air and brought them to Adam for Adam to name them. But for Adam there was no helper comparable to him. Then the LORD God made deep sleep to fall upon Adam and took one of his ribs, closed up the flesh in its place, and made the rib into a woman and brought her to him. Adam called her Woman as she was taken out of Man. Adam realised that Woman was now bone of his bones and flesh of his flesh. Therefore man shall leave his father and mother and shall cling to his wife and they shall become one flesh.
6. State [Gen 2:25]: The man and his wife were both naked but not ashamed.

Meditation Notes
Entities
....
....
....

Questions
....
....
....

Exploration Areas
....
....
....

II. Beginnings

Cross References
....
....
....…

Other Points
....
....
....…

Reference Notes
(iii) Entities
The LORD God, man, woman, beasts of the field and bird of the air, Eden, garden in/of Eden, Pishon, Gihon, Hiddekel, Euphrates, Havilah, Cush, Assyria, gold, Bdellium, onyx, tree of life, tree of knowledge of good and evil.

(v) Name of God
LORD God (Yodh-hey-vav-hey 'elohıym, יְהוָֹה אֱלֹהִים).

(vi) Deeper Questions
(1) We have two accounts of creation - one in Genesis 1:1-2:3 and another in Genesis 2:4-2:25. How do we know the former is a chronological account and the latter is a topical account?

Genesis 1:1-2:3 has details of creation arranged in periods described as days which are qualified as 'the evening and the morning', 'the first', 'Day and Night' [Gen 1:5 etc] leading us to understand that these periods are literal days. Further more, the ordinal numbers 'first', 'second' etc in 'the first day' [Gen 1:5] etc clearly enables us place the days in contiguous, chronological order.

Genesis 2:4-2:25 on the other hand can be understood to be not a chronological arrangement because of two reasons.

(a) Absence of qualification of 'yom' and any ordinal description: This passage begins with a brief presentation of the reference time (for the description of creation that is to follow), 'in the day that the LORD God made the earth and the heavens', 'before any plant of the field was in the earth and before any herb of the field had grown'. Please note that in 'in the day that the LORD God made the earth and the heavens', 'the day' (Hebrew

The Old World

term 'yom' (yôm, יוֹם)) would be more accurately rendered as 'the time' (as in 'in my grand father's time') which is a descriptor of an arbitrary length of time (Please see section II.A.vi.9). This is because this 'yom' is not qualified any further, unlike in Genesis 1:1-2:3, either with specific detail of how this yom relates to day and night or evening and morning, or with an ordinal description.

(b) Repeated ideas in different places: In this passage you can see ideas repeated like '... in Eden ... He put the man whom He had formed' [Gen 2:8] and 'the LORD God took the man and put him in the garden of Eden' [Gen 2:15] separated by a description of different things. In other words, the author seems to have taken the liberty to not care about chronological order.

(2) Genesis 1:1-2:3 uses the term God ('elohıym, אֱלֹהִים) while Genesis 2:4-2:25 uses the term LORD God (Yodh-hey-vav-hey 'elohıym, יְהוָה אֱלֹהִים). Why could this be?

Genesis 1:1-2:3 seems like an impassioned chronological account of creation whereas Genesis 2:4-2:25 is a passionate topical account of how the LORD God created things with man in the centre. The usages of 'God' ('elohıym, אֱלֹהִים) (an impassionate matter-of-fact reference of the entity behind creation) and 'LORD God' (Yodh-hey-vav-hey 'elohıym, יְהוָה אֱלֹהִים) (a deeply personal and relational name revealed personally only to specific people in the history of the world) in Genesis 1:1-2:3 and Genesis 2:4-2:25 respecively seems to reflect the difference in attitudes in the 2 accounts.

(3) Could there be a difference between herb [Gen 1:11] and herb of the field [Gen 2:5] and similarly beast [Gen 1:25] and beast of the field [Gen 2:19]?

It is possible that the herbs referred to in Genesis 2:5 is a subset of the herbs referred to in Genesis 1:11 because of the further qualification of herbs available in Genesis 2:5 ('of the field'). A similar reasoning applies to beasts referred to in Genesis 1:25 and Genesis 2:19 also. Please note that - both of the above are only possibilities which need not be true and even if not has no bearing on the consistency of Genesis 1:1-2:3 and Genesis 2:4-2:25 accounts of creation.

(4) Man was said to have been formed from the 'dust of the ground' [Gen 2:7] while the animals were formed from the 'ground' [Gen 2:19]. Is the

II. Beginnings

'dust of the ground' different from the 'ground'?
It is perhaps possible that the 'dust of the ground' is different from merely 'ground'.

(5) How exactly did man become a 'living being' [Gen 2:7]?
The LORD God 'formed' man of the 'dust of the ground' - this is perhaps related to the physical components of man. Then the LORD God 'breathed' into his nostrils the breath of life and man became a 'living being' - this gives the non-physical component 'life' to man.

(6) Where is Eden? Did the LORD God put a garden in Eden meaning Eden could have been more than just the garden [Gen 2:8]?
Descriptions like 'garden eastward in Eden', 'river went out of Eden to water the garden' may seem to suggest that the garden where Adam was put in was only a small portion of Eden.

(7) Were the tree of life and tree of knowledge of good and evil created as part of the creation week? Were they pleasant to the sight and good for food?
From the way the trees are presented in Genesis 2:9, it may seem as if the tree of life and tree of the knowledge of good and evil are mentioned 'as an aside' and 'apart from the created trees'. Please note that this is only a possibility and even if this were true, the origin(s) of these trees is(are) not clarified.

(8) Should someone need to know what evil is to understand good?
It is not true that someone should know evil to understand good as much as someone can know for himself that he is alive before he dies. In creation, Adam already was experiencing 'good' in that he was experiencing God and his creative acts. He didn't have to know what evil is to go through this experience.

It is however true that if we are not wise enough, we would need to know evil to appreciate good as much as the fact that someone may begin to appreciate life when he gets to know about death.

(9) Where is the river / and its river heads which went out of Eden via the garden to outside the garden again?

The Old World

A river went out of Eden to water the garden and from there parted and became four riverheads - Pishon, Gihon, Hiddekel/Tigris and Euphrates. Two of the river heads survive today as Tigris and Euphrates, although not necessarily in the original form. Please note that the Bible goes on to talk about a cataclysmic, world wide flood during the time of Noah [Gen 7:11-7:12, Gen 7:17-7:21] and therefore we should not be surprised to not see pre-Noahic rivers today.

(10) Why was man created? How does that purpose sit with the task assigned to Adam? Why was woman created?

According to Genesis 1:26, man was created in the image of God and in His likeness. He was created to have dominion over the fish of the sea, over the birds of the air, and over all the cattle, over all the earth and over every creeping thing that creeps on the earth. An implicit point here is that God seems to have wanted to nurture someone just 'like him' to take up a role which otherwise would have been His (God created and therefore would be the automatic being to have dominion over all creation) - this in other words means that God wanted someone to come alongside Him. This by no means would undermine the fact that He is still the creator of man and therefore would expect reverence from the man.

According to Genesis 2:15, the LORD God put the man to tend and keep the garden which is consistent with the broader object as discussed above.

Woman, on the other hand was created as a 'comparable', 'helper' for the man [Gen 2:18]. Having been created to be 'comparable' and to be a 'helper' to man, it is not hard to understand that the woman was asked to partner with the man in all the purpose which the LORD God had for the man.

(11) Who was given the commandment related to the eating of the fruit of the knowledge of good and evil? Was it Adam alone or both Adam and Woman?

In the topical arrangement of creation account as presented in Genesis 2:4-2:25, the commandment given related to the eating of the fruit of the knowledge of good and evil is presented only in regards to Adam [Gen 2:15-2:17]. This either meant the LORD God had commanded only Adam or at the least means the LORD God expected Adam to be ultimately responsible for the keeping of the commandment.

II. Beginnings

(12) If before eating of the tree of knowledge of good and evil a person does not have the knowledge of good and evil, on what basis is Adam supposed to obey the commandment?

Before eating the tree of knowledge of good and evil it is true that Adam would not have the knowledge to differentiate between good and evil by the fact of not knowing what evil is (Please see the discussion for question 8). However, what he had at that time is the knowledge that the LORD God was the reason for his existence. On top of this, all he needed was obedience to the one who is the reason for his existence to perfectly remain within the boundaries of life even without knowing an inkling of the difference between good and evil.

(13) When was Adam named? Who named him?

Man is referred to as Adam for the first time in Genesis 2:19. This is in the passage which goes on to describe how Adam named every beast of the field and every bird of the air. In this context, it is not hard to imagine that the LORD God had named man as Adam first sometime before the beasts and birds were named by Adam.

(14) Did Adam have to name millions of beasts of the field and birds of the air?

Genesis 2:19-20 states that Adam named all the beasts of the field and the birds of the air. Please note that the number of beasts and birds that he would have named might not have run into the millions. In the creation account, the LORD God talks about 'kinds' [Gen 1:21, 24] and not 'species' as we identify. The number of 'kinds' required to produce all the 'species' that we have today would have been only in the few thousands. Naming all these might have been a manageable experience.

(15) When was language introduced?

A system of intelligent communication should have been in place for the LORD God to communicate a specific command [Gen 2:16-2:17] to Adam. Furthermore it seems like Adam had chosen a name for the woman with a specific meaning in a system of representation [Gen 2:23]. In other words, the LORD God had not alone created a grown up individual in Adam but also introduced to him a sophisticated language.

(16) Did the LORD God expect to find a helper comparable to man from the animals?

The Old World

It is curious to see how the narrative of finding a 'helper comparable' to man is presented in Genesis 2:18-2:20. The passage begins with the identified need and finishes off by the unfulfilled need. What had happened in between was that Adam named all the animals. In this context, it is not an over stretch to imagine that perhaps the LORD God tried to see if Adam considered any of the animals as a 'helper comparable' to him.

(17) Who introduced the institution of marriage? What are the essential components to this institution?

The LORD God had first introduced the institution of marriage in creating a woman to be a helper comparable to the man.

The essential components to this institution are -

- An appropriate choice being made to determine who will be a 'helper comparable' to a man is [Gen 2:18, 2:20]
- Participation of the LORD God in an overseeing mode on the selection of the helper, with the choice somewhat left to the man also (Please see the discussion for question 16)
- Woman being recognized both as a 'helper' and as 'comparable' to man in nature [Gen 2:18, 2:20]
- Man and the chosen woman to be united as one flesh [Gen 2:24], with the man leaving his father and mother for the sake of being united with his wife

(18) Was there an idea of childbirth soon after Adam and Woman were created?

It is curious to note a couple of important points in the account about Adam and the woman before sin entered in to the world.

- The man and his wife were both naked but not ashamed [Gen 2:25].
- The wife's name was just woman and not Eve (the 'mother of all living') [Gen 2:23] and absence of any attempt to have children.

Please also note that despite the fact that God wanted Adam and his wife to be 'fruitful' and 'multiply' and 'fill' the earth and 'subdue' it [Gen 1:28], no specific instruction of childbirth seems to have been given. Please also note that there is nothing (apart from our hindsight knowledge, after the fall, about reproduction) to suggest that God was even talking about necessarily more humans filling the earth. In all probability the words ('fruitful' etc) would be fulfilled if Adam and his wife reared and

II. Beginnings

enabled the animals to reproduce more or even plant new gardens etc. Lastly, please also note that even if God had intended the man and the woman to reproduce, this reproduction need not necessarily have been through physical consummation after getting to know the nakedness of each other. For instance in the case of the Emmanuel, He was conceived when the Spirit of the Lord overshadowed Mary [Matt 1:18, Luke 1:34-1:35] - it is not hard to imagine that something similar is a possibility in the case between Adam and the woman.

The Old World

III
Pause & Consider - How Was Creation Before Man's Fall?

'Thus says the Lord God: "On the day that I cleanse you from all your iniquities, I will also enable you to dwell in the cities, and the ruins shall be rebuilt. The desolate land shall be tilled instead of lying desolate in the sight of all who pass by. So they will say, 'This land that was desolate has become like the garden of Eden; and the wasted, desolate, and ruined cities are now fortified and inhabited.' Then the nations which are left all around you shall know that I, the Lord, have rebuilt the ruined places and planted what was desolate. I, the Lord, have spoken it, and I will do it."'

Ezekiel 36:33-36:36

Adam was at the centre of God's attention in creation. God had intended Adam to be a steward over all creation. What would rightly be under the authority and stewardship of God (owing to the fact that all creation derived its reason of existence in God), was commended in the hands of Adam. In other words, God was nurturing Adam to be like God in the areas where it is possible to be like God. God was deeply involved in the life of Adam in a very supportive and friendly way.

God had placed a garden in Eden. Adam's headquarters was in the garden. Adam began his stewardship with a reasonably well defined job role - he was supposed to tend and keep the garden. God also had implicitly clarified that he also was supposed to take care of all the animals. This was clarified through the act that God brought all animals to Adam for Adam to name them.

All provisions that Adam would have needed was placed in the garden - water and variety of food. To surround him with riches, God had also placed precious metals and stones like gold, bdellium, onyx in his reach. Close companionship and help was provided to him, through the woman who was made from Adam.

Adam was provided the best possible opportunity to have a very

The Old World

meaningful life filled with love, companionship, friendship, helping hand, provisions, stress free and rewarding work, responsibility and respect. Things that clutter a modern day human's life like worry, stress, pain, suffering, work-life imbalance etc were not a problem at all for Adam.

There were other prominent things that we take for granted that were absent.

Death was the crucial thing which was missing. Adam was supposed to live forever, with God, the woman and the rest of creation.

Carnivores tendency was absent entirely also. God had given all fresh herbs and trees as sources of food for man and all fresh herbs as sources of food for animals. All animals were domestic.

In regards to the land, thorns and thistles were notably absent also {Gen 3:18} and the ground was very productive and amenable for high plant yield {Gen 3:17}.

Adam and the woman were the only human beings on the face of all the earth. There was no immediate urge to reproduce and have children.

There was a simple moral compass - a single commandment - which was for Adam not to eat of the tree of knowledge of good and evil. This simple moral compass would enable Adam to live a life of innocence without having to explore and be soiled with evil. This simple moral compass would also provide an objective measure of saying if Adam was being faithful to the one who he knows to be the reason of his existence.

IV
Fall

"For the creation was subjected to futility, not willingly, but because of Him who subjected it in hope"
Romans 8:20-8:21

A. Deception & Disobedience

(i) Bible Passage - Genesis 3:1-3:11

(ii) Summary

1. Doubt [Gen 3:1]: The most cunning beast of the field, the serpent, starts a conversation with the woman by sowing doubt about God's commandment - "Has God indeed said, 'you shall not eat of every tree of the garden'?"

2. Deception [Gen 3:2-3:6]: The woman engages in the conversation with the serpent - 'We may eat the fruit of the trees of the garden; but of the fruit of the tree which is in the midst of the garden, God has said, 'you shall not eat it, nor shall you touch it, lest you die'. The serpent responded with a lie - 'you will not surely die' and added - 'for God knows that in the day you eat of it your eyes will be opened and you will be like God, knowing good and evil'. The woman saw that the tree was good for food, that it was pleasant to the eyes and a tree desirable to make one wise and she took its fruit and ate it.

3. Disobedience [Gen 3:6]: Adam also ate of the tree of knowledge of good and evil, when the woman gave it to her husband who was with her.

4. Automatic Consequence [Gen 3:7-11]:

    a. Eyes opened [Gen 3:7]: Eyes of both Adam and the woman were opened and they knew they were naked.

    b. Shame [Gen 3:7]: They sewed fig leaves together and made themselves coverings.

    c. Fear & separation from LORD God [Gen 3:8-10]: Adam

The Old World

and his wife hid themselves when they heard the sound of the LORD God because they were afraid that they were naked. This is despite the fig coverings that they had made.

Meditation Notes

Entities

....
....
....

Questions

....
....
....

Exploration Areas

....
....
....

Cross References

....
....
....

Other Points

....
....
....

Reference Notes

(iii) Entities

The LORD God, serpent, trees of the garden, tree of knowledge of good and evil, the woman, Adam.

(vi) Deeper Questions

(1) If the serpent was part of creation [Gen 3:1] which was acknowledged by God to be good [Gen 1:25] how did it become an agent of evil?

We do not know the precise motivation of the serpent in deceiving the woman. We can however surmise:

- The motivation might have been 'negative' - to disrupt the order in

IV. Fall

creation, with God being the ultimate authority, man being the person with dominion on the earth and every beast (including the serpent) being subject to the man on the earth.

- Alternatively, the motivation could have been 'neutral' - to just find out what would happen if man disobeys.

Regardless of the motivation, what is clear is that the action of the serpent essentially undermined God's authority and truth. The tools that the devil also used are either deliberate lies or twisted, partial and skewed evaluation of the facts.

What also needs to be appreciated is that the mere presence of the faculty of free choice does not make a created being bad (This would have applied to the serpent to begin with). However, such a 'good' being can 'choose' to turn evil out of its own volition. In other words, what may be 'good' during creation can turn 'bad' through a 'bad' choice exercised using a morally neutral faculty called 'free choice'.

(2) Was the woman's idea of the commandment right?

For some reason the woman's idea of the commandment was not entirely accurate. The woman thought that she is not supposed to even touch the fruit of the tree of knowledge of good and evil [Gen 3:3]. This was not part of the commandment. This either means the commandment was embellished by human ideas either by the woman or by the man, which may or may not have increased the possibility of deception.

(3) What portions of the serpent's communication are lies?

The serpent communicated a few specific points about the fruit of the tree of knowledge of good and evil. Some of them are true and some of them aren't.

True statements:

- God knows that in the day you eat of it your eyes will be opened' [Gen 3:5, 3:7]
- You will be like God, knowing good and evil' [Gen 3:5, 3:7]

Lies:

- You will not surely die' [Gen 3:4] in contrary to Genesis 2:17
- God knows that in the day you eat of it your eyes will be opened' [Gen 3:5, 3:7] somehow portrays 'eyes opening' as some sort of

privilege and also communicates that God just didn't like this privilege to be vested upon man.

(4) What was the criteria used by the woman to eat of the tree of knowledge of good and evil? What was the problem with this evaluation?
The woman decided to eat of the tree of knowledge of good and evil based on the following criteria
- good for food
- pleasant to the eyes
- desirable to make one wise

There is a main problem here. She omitted the most crucial criterion - God's input - which is that eating this would result in death [Gen 2:17]. If only she had this in her mind properly, the rest of the points will either fade in comparison (how does the looks of the fruit matter if the consequence of eating it is death?) or will show up as plain nonsensical (how can eating to die be wise?). It is carefully to be noted that the serpent did not bring this point up at all - so part of the serpent's deception is to hide the truth.

The simple thumb rules that must have been used in the woman's decision making -
- Consider all the competing inputs.
- Trust the inputs that are from a person who have a track record of trustworthiness even if that means going against someone else's input.

(5) Where was Adam when the woman had decided to eat? What should he have done about the woman eating of the tree of knowledge of good and evil?
From the usage of the term 'with her' [Gen 3:6], it seems like Adam was near the woman when she ate the fruit. He should have advised the woman to not eat and perhaps should have even rebuked the serpent for twisting the facts.

(6) What is the difference between Adam eating the fruit and the woman eating the fruit?
Adam was given the command about the tree of the knowledge of the good

IV. Fall

and evil and the woman was not [Gen 2:15-2:18, 2:21-2:22]. At the least he was given the primary responsibility to obey the command. So - when Adam ate despite the command it would be considered disobedience. This will not apply to the woman.

(7) How do we know the LORD God was in fellowship with Adam and the woman in the garden?

When the sound of the LORD God walking in the garden was heard, Adam and the woman knew that it was the LORD God [Gen 3:8]. This indicates to us that the LORD God has walked in the garden enough number of times in the garden for them to be familiar and to be able to identify it was Him.

(8) If the LORD God knows all things (omniscient) why did He ask 'where are you'?

It is important to understand that a question asked does not necessarily mean the questioner has no answer to the question. It only means the questioner wants an answer from the questionee (the one to whom the question is asked).

(9) Why did Adam and the woman hide themselves?

The basic reason is fear [Gen 3:10]. The curious thing is however, Adam said he was afraid because he was naked as opposed to being afraid because he did something the LORD God did not want him to do. This can possibly mean that he had the wrong reason for being afraid. This can however alternatively mean that Adam got to know the truth behind the LORD God's advice [Gen 2:17], through the enormity of the new knowledge which they acquired (knowing that they were naked) as a result of eating the fruit.

(10) How was the LORD God able to immediately connect the knowledge of nakedness [Gen 3:10] with the eating of the forbidden fruit [Gen 3:11]?

Initially the man and the woman were not ashamed of the nakedness [Gen 2:25]. Eating the forbidden fruit not only made them ashamed [Gen 3:7] but also afraid [Gen 3:10]. This essentially means that Adam and the woman were able to interpret nakedness in a specific negative way which they hadn't done before. This seemingly was possible only when they had knowledge of good and evil, which comes through eating the forbidden.

B. Judgment

(i) Bible Passage - Genesis 3:11-3:21

The Old World

(ii) Summary
1. The blame game [Gen 3:11-3:13]: The LORD God asked Adam (who was the one ultimately responsible to keep the commandment [Gen 2:16-17]) if he ate of the tree of knowledge of good and evil. Adam responded by answering an unasked question by saying it was the woman who gave the fruit to him. When the woman was asked about her motivation she responded by saying that she was deceived by the serpent.
2. Judgment on the serpent [Gen 3:14-3:15]:
   a. Reason: The serpent was judged because the serpent deceived [Gen 3:13-3:14].
   b. Curse: LORD God cursed more than all the cattle and all the beasts of the field [Gen 3:14].
   c. Locomotion: The serpent shall move on its belly [Gen 3:14].
   d. Dust: The serpent shall eat dust all the days of its life [Gen 3:14].
   e. Enmity: Enmity between the serpent and the woman, the seed of the serpent and the seed of the woman [Gen 3:15].
   f. End: The seed of the woman shall bruise the serpent's head and the serpent shall bruise His heel [Gen 3:15].
3. Judgment on the woman [Gen 3:16]:
   a. Reason: The woman was deceived [Gen 3:13].
   b. Sorrow: LORD God shall greatly multiply sorrow [Gen 3:16].
   c. Conception: LORD God shall greatly multiply conception [Gen 3:16].
   d. Pain: Pain during childbirth [Gen 3:16].
   e. Subject: Desire for the husband but the husband shall rule over her [Gen 3:16].
4. Judgment on Adam [Gen 3:17-3:19]:
   a. Reason: Adam disobeyed the LORD God's commandment [Gen 3:17].
   b. The LORD God points out that it was to Adam the com

IV. Fall

mandment was given [Gen 3:17].
  c. Curse: The ground was cursed for Adam's sake [Gen 3:17].
  d. Hard labour: Man had to toil going forward to eat of the ground [Gen 3:17] and will have to sweat to get his bread [Gen 3:18].
  e. Pain: Thorns and thistles the ground shall bring forth [Gen 3:18].
  f. No garden: Man will have eat from the herb of the field going forward as opposed to the fruit of the various trees [Gen 3:18].
  g. Death: Man will return to the ground [Gen 3:19].
5. The woman becomes Eve [Gen 3:20]: Because the idea of conception was introduced to the woman (and Adam), Adam called his wife Eve (meaning 'life giver').
6. Temporary cover for the shame [Gen 3:21]: The LORD God made tunics of skin and clothed Adam and Eve.

Meditation Notes
Entities
....
....
....
Questions
....
....
....
Exploration Areas
....
....
....
Cross References
....
....
....

The Old World

Other Points

....

....

....

Reference Notes

(iii) Entities

The LORD God, the serpent, the woman, the man, the tree of life, Cherubim, flaming sword.

(vi) Deeper Questions

(1) The woman was deceived and Adam disobeyed? What is the difference? Why did God judge only Adam in regards to the disobedience?

It was to Adam the commandment forbidding the eating of the fruit of the tree of knowledge of good and evil given [Gen 2:16-17] (Please see section II.B.vi.11).

The serpent could engage on the conversation only with the woman. The serpent was further able to, by lying, twisting the truth and introducing a partial evaluation of the truth etc able to convince the woman that she should eat the forbidden fruit. The woman was genuinely led to think that eating the fruit was going to benefit her ('good for food', 'pleasant to the eyes' and 'desirable to make one wise' [Gen 3:6]).

In contrast to the woman, there is no indication Adam was led to think that eating the fruit was going to benefit him. In spite of this, he went ahead and ate the fruit contrary to the commandment, perhaps just to please the woman ('because you have heeded the voice of your wife' [Gen 3:17]). This is a deliberate act of flouting of the commandment (disobedience).

(2) What do we understand about the initial nature of the serpent? What do we understand about its fallen nature?

'On your belly shall you go' [Gen 3:14] tells us that the serpent moving on its belly is a consequence of its part in deceiving the woman.

'I will put enmity between you and the woman, and between your seed and her Seed' [Gen 3:15] tells us that prior to the fall there was no automatic animosity between the serpent and the woman.

(3) Does the serpent eat dust?

A snake has an organ called the Jacobson's organ located in the front of the roof of its mouth that functions as a chemical receptor. The Jacobson's

IV. Fall

organ helps the snake smell. As a snake's forked tongue darts out to sense its surroundings, it, at least occasionally, licks the ground or picks up dust particles. Once the snake pulls in its tongue, it inserts the tips of its forked tongue into the two openings of the Jacobson's organ, where the particles are identified and analyzed. The snake's brain can "read" the smells and tastes from its tongue. So, in a way, snakes really do eat dust. (Courtesy: Answers in Genesis).

(4) What is the enmity between the serpent and the woman? What is the enmity between the serpent's seed and the woman's Seed? What does bruising someone's head and heel mean?

Prior to the fall, every created being seemed to have lived a harmonious life with each other. Animals were herbivores [Gen 1:29-1:30].

It seems like during the fall, the LORD God puts in animosity between the serpent and the woman and the seed of the serpent and the Seed of the woman [Gen 3:15]. Please note that the word used 'seed' is in the singular and therefore refers to specific individuals from among the descendants of both the serpent and the woman. As a matter of fact one of the New Testament writers, Paul goes on to expand how this Seed of the woman was the Messiah. It is however interesting also note that the LORD God says the Seed of the woman (and not the woman) will bruise the serpent (and not the seed of the serpent). In other words, the LORD seems to assume that the serpent was going to be alive long enough for the Messiah to come later and bruise his head and that it was this serpent which is the problem and not the seed of the serpent. This is not surprising when we understand that the LORD God elsewhere in scripture also in a seamless way addresses the spirits behind physical entities by directly addressing the physical entities who have given room for the spiritual entities.

(5) Is increase in conception itself a punishment for the woman? Without the fall of man would human population have grown to an extent it has now?

Please note that 'increase in sorrow' and 'increase in conception' are part of the punishments given to the woman as a result of her part in the fall [Gen 3:16] apart from the a couple of other things. Prior to this, the man and the woman seemed not to have contemplated about having children. It is perhaps not an overstretch to say that if not for the fall, perhaps it might have just been Adam and the woman (and she wouldn't have become Eve [Gen 3:20]) who would still inhabit the earth and therefore there wouldn't

The Old World

be scarcity of natural resources etc.

(6) How is the relationship between man and his wife affected as a result of the judgment?

As a result of the fall, the woman's desire shall be for her husband and he shall rule over her [Gen 3:16]. Please note that a similar statement is used in relation to sin and Cain - sin's desire is for you but Cain was supposed to rule over it [Gen 4:7].

'The woman's desire shall be for her husband' very likely means that the woman may want to subordinate/consume/take over her husband (much like how sin can subordinate/consume/take over a man), which when put in a polite way may mean that a woman may want her husband to live for her.

'He shall rule over her' very likely means that the husband may have an intrinsic domineering attitude which results in domineering actions.

Both these actions (from the husband and the wife) are because of the fall and are penalties from the LORD God. If not for the fall, the LORD God would have wanted the husband and wife to have lived together for God in an effective partnership, where both are 'comparable' and the wife was going to 'help' the husband [Gen 2:18].

(7) What must Adam do, after the disobedience, to feed himself and his wife?

To feed themselves, Adam, after the fall, had to 'toil' [Gen 3:17], till [Gen 3:23], deal with thorns and thistles [Gen 3:18] and sweat [Gen 3:19].

(8) Did the earth have thorns and thistles before the fall of man?

It seems like all thorns and thistles were a result of sin of man [Gen 3:18]. It is not an overstretch to assume that before the fall the earth produced only pleasant herbs and trees.

(9) God had warned 'in the day that you eat of it you shall surely die' [Gen 2:17]. Did this happen?

On multiple levels death was indeed introduced on the same day as the disobedience.

Access to life refused:

- Tree of life not to be accessible by Adam and the woman [Gen 3:22]

IV. Fall

- Presence of God, the ultimate source of life, in Adam's life, is very likely diminished. Prior to the fall, God came to the garden to have fellowship with Adam and the woman [Gen 3:8]. There is no indication that God had such a fellowship with Adam and the woman outside the garden.

Exposed to the elements:

- After the disobedience, Adam was going to be exposed to the elements like heat [Gen 3:19], aridness, thorns and thistles [Gen 3:18], which will have an impact on Adam's life if not properly countered.

(10) Was the LORD sacrificing an animal, part of his original intention?

If Adam and the woman hadn't fallen, there is no need to kill an animal. In other words, when Adam and the woman had fallen, what could have legitimately enjoyed a proper, long life, was in the entire sense of the word 'sacrificed' for the man.

To understand how the idea of 'sacrifice' was communicated to Adam, we must observe the following. God had communicated that on the day Adam eats of the tree of knowledge of good and evil he shall surely die [Gen 2:17]. On the day when Adam did eat, Adam immediately realised that drastic changes happened to him, as he came to know that he was naked [Gen 3:7]. This is change in infinite degree as someone who knew no issue is now getting to know at least one issue. This must have reminded him of the fact of the death that God had warned him about. This must have terrified Adam [Gen 3:10] and made him wonder what more could happen to him (as he wouldn't have had practical experience of death before). It is in this context, that the LORD God kills an animal to deal with the issue that Adam had (i.e. nakedness). Adam must have realised that for no sin of it the animal was killed and that this meant Adam could still 'survive' - this must be a clear communication of vicarious sacrifice to Adam in implicit terms.

(vii) Explore

(1) Adam And Eve Seal:

There is a seal found, dating back to about 2200-2100 BC, originating from Ur (Third dynasty of Ur or Akkadian), which shows a man, a woman, a tree and serpents bearing high degree of overlap with the Biblical account of Adam, Eve, the tree of knowledge of good and evil and the serpent.

The Old World

Figure 7 - Adam And Eve Seal

Courtesy: British Museum

(2) Serpent In Different Cultures:

A serpent is one of the oldest and widest mythological symbols - often signifying either fertility, an umbilical cord or simply denoting the mysteries of birth and regeneration. This has a high degree of overlap with the fact that during the fall (as induced by the serpent), the LORD pronounced judgement on Eve and said 'I will greatly multiply your sorrow and childbirth'.

C. Life Outside the Garden

(i) Bible Passage - Genesis 3:22-3:24

(ii) Summary

1. Difficulty for the LORD God [Gen 3:22]: The LORD God could not let someone who knew good and evil to eat from the tree of life also. So the LORD God sent Adam and Eve out of the garden.
2. Change in work [Gen 3:23]: The LORD God required Adam now to till the ground.
3. Garden of Eden's entry protected [Gen 3:24]: The LORD God placed a cherubim east of the garden of Eden and a flaming sword to guard the way to the tree of life.

IV. Fall

Meditation Notes
Entities
....
....
....

Questions
....
....
....

Exploration Areas
....
....
....

Cross References
....
....
....

Other Points
....
....
....

Reference Notes

(iii) Entities

The LORD God, tree of life, Cherubim, flaming sword.

(vi) Deeper Questions

(1) If God is so loving why did God not like man eating from the tree of life also, regardless of whether he knows good and evil or not?

When Adam and the woman had eaten the forbidden fruit, the LORD God recognizes that 'the man has become like one of us to know good and evil' and He seems not to want to the man 'to take also from the tree of life, and eat, and live forever [Gen 3:22].

This may, unless properly examined make us come to inappropriate conclusions about the LORD God's plan for man.

The Old World

We need to understand the following
- The LORD God didn't want to damn man because of his disobedience and as a matter of fact to the contrary he wanted to redeem man [Gen 3:15]
- The LORD God was willing to sacrifice an animal for man [Gen 3:21]
- It is only in the knowledge of good and evil God acknowledged man had become like God [Gen 3:22]. In other words, when the LORD God says 'the man has become like one of us to know good and evil ...', this does not indicate jealousy as God would be different (and superior) to man in multiple other ways. However, having knowledge of good and evil without some of the other attributes like holiness, perfection etc is a problem (to the wider community) and not a privilege. God hence did not want man to live forever in this problematic state.

(2) What precisely changed in Adam's employment as a result of the fall?

Prior to the fall, Adam had the enviable job of being the manager of a very rich, well watered garden. All that he had to do was to tend the garden and to keep it [Gen 2:15]. He was allowed to eat from all but one tree in the garden.

After the fall, Adam had to till the ground [Gen 3:23].

(3) Where are the cherubim and the flaming sword that the LORD God had placed east of the garden of Eden today? As a matter of fact where is the garden of Eden today?

The location of the garden of Eden and the cherubim and the flaming sword is not known today. Please note that the Bible goes on to talk about a cataclysmic, world wide flood during the time of Noah [Gen 7:11-7:12, Gen 7:17-7:21] and therefore we do not necessarily expect to see all the features during the time of Adam today.

V
Pause & Consider - How Was Creation After Man's Fall?

"...For we know that the whole creation groans and labors with birth pangs together until now."
Romans 8:22

God had given a simple moral compass to Adam - a single commandment - which was not to eat the tree of knowledge of good and evil.

The immediate consequence of eating of the tree of knowledge of good and evil is receiving knowledge to distinguish between good and evil. In other words, who was prior to this supposed to live an innocent life of bliss, is now going have to deal with the enormity of knowledge of evil also and the temptation to commit evil. Adam and the woman got to immediately know that they were naked.

More than the acquisition of the knowledge of nakedness there were other consequences also, because of the changes God wanted to bring in.

It is important to note that Adam was not deceived to eat of the tree of knowledge of good and evil unlike the woman i.e. he was not convinced that eating the fruit was going to be beneficial for him. In other words, his act of eating from the tree of knowledge of good and evil was an act of deliberate disobedience.

When Adam disobeyed God in the single commandment, there was a rift between him and God. Adam became someone who had deliberately disobeyed once and therefore who could deliberately disobey in the future. In other words, God had to bring in appropriate changes to the system in place.

The changes that God brought in were in multiple levels.

Firstly, there were a few different changes in the relational level. Although God's presence was not entirely taken away from Adam {Gen 4:16} and the woman, seemingly they were not going to have a profound fellowship with God as they used to have. Also, before the fall, Adam and the woman were 'comparable' and the woman, even though being from the

The Old World

man, was of a calibre, to an extent that, she was going to help Adam {Gen 2:18}. After the fall, the woman was going to long to be at the centre of her husband's attention, but the man shall rule over the woman.

Secondly, God also had introduced changes on the level of provisions. The earth was cursed to be not as productive as it used to be and it was going to bear thorns and thistles. Adam and the woman were forced to toil for their daily bread. The access to easily available food (garden of Eden) was removed from them.

Thirdly, God introduced death. God hadn't originally intended man to have death. Death was however introduced as a result of Adam's disobedience so that evil can be managed and (at least temporarily) removed when a man is tempted by his knowledge of sin to explore and practice sin.

Fourthly, the knowledge of nakedness brought in an apparent immediate interest in sexual reproduction. The woman was renamed as Eve (mother of all the living) by Adam in recognition of the fact that Adam now saw the woman as a mother also (owing to his ideas about reproduction).

VI
Spread Of Sin

" ...just as through one man sin entered the world, and death through sin, and thus death spread to all men, because all sinned" Romans 5:12

A. Murder & Curse

(i) Bible Passage - Genesis 4:1-4:15

(ii) Summary

1. Children & professions [Gen 4:1-4:2]: Adam and Eve bore Cain (Cain means 'acquired' or 'spear'). Eve named the son Cain to signify that she had gotten a man from the LORD. Then Eve bore again and she had Abel (Abel means 'breath'). Cain was a tiller of the ground and Abel, a keeper of sheep.
2. Offerings & the LORD's response [Gen 4:3-4:5]: Cain brought an offering of the fruit of the ground to the LORD and Abel brought an offering of the firstlings of the flock and their fat. The LORD respected Abel's offering but not Cain's. Cain was angry because of this.
3. Mechanism of sin [Gen 4:6-4:7]: The LORD said - 'if you do well, will you not be accepted? but if you do not do well, sin lies at the door. Its desire is for you but you should rule over it'.
4. Murder [Gen 4:8]: Cain did not rule over the sin and he ended up talking to his brother Abel and when they were in the field, Cain rose against his brother and killed him.
5. Irresponsible behaviour [Gen 4:9]: God asked Cain where Abel was implying that he expected Cain to know it. Cain responded by asking if was his brother's keeper.
6. Blood [Gen 4:10]: The voice of the blood of Abel cried out to God from the earth and the LORD wanted to get an account of what had happened.
7. Curse [Gen 4:11-4:12]: Cain was cursed from the earth which received Abel's blood. The earth was not going to yield its strength to Cain. Cain was also going to be fugitive and vagabond on the earth.
8. Mark on Cain [Gen 4:13-Gen 4:14]: Cain understood that his

The Old World

punishment was greater than what he can bear and that someone who finds him may kill him. The LORD committed to punish someone who kills Cain even sevenfold and set a mark on Cain so that anyone who finds him should not kill him.

Meditation Notes

Entities

....
....
....

Questions

....
....
....

Exploration Areas

....
....
....

Cross References

....
....
....

Other Points

....
....
....

Reference Notes

(iii) Entities

The LORD, Adam, Eve, Cain, Abel

(vi) Deeper Questions

(1) Who gave Cain and Abel the idea that the LORD liked offerings?

It is not clear how Cain and Abel came to the understanding that the LORD God liked offerings.

When Adam and the woman had disobeyed, God had sacrificed an animal (or multiple animals) to clothe Adam and the woman. Adam who

VI. Spread Of Sin

would have anticipated to receive death might have seen that in the sacrifice of the animal, his death was being delayed. He might have picked a cue from here about the idea about an 'offering'.

It is also not an overstretch to imagine that the LORD God in communicating to Adam and Eve after the fall and Cain and Abel after they were born, admonished them to trust and have faith in Him or even suggested that they offer their produce as a way of proving their faith in Him.

(2) Why was Cain's offering not accepted while Abel's was accepted?

'By faith Abel offered to God a more excellent sacrifice than Cain' [Hebrews 11:4].

Cain brought an offering from the fruit of the ground to the LORD. Abel also brought of the firstlings of his flock and of their fat. The LORD respected Abel and his offering but He did not respect Cain and his offering. [Gen 4:3-4:5].

The precise reason as to why Abel's offering was considered more excellent is not explicitly mentioned. However, we see at least that Abel offered from the 'firstlings' of his flock. Normally when you offer the firstling it means you offer the first produce right after the produce (i.e. offer all the produce so far) and trusting God to give back. On the other hand there is nothing to indicate Cain did something similar.

(3) What was wrong in Cain's response to God's rejection of his offering?

When God rejected Cain's offering, Cain's countenance fell and he was angry [Gen 4:5]. This is unreasonable. When God rejects a unworthy offering, the problem is the unworthiness of the offering and not the rejection. So an appropriate response would only be for Cain to have repented and given a more suitable offering as opposed to being angry as if he was wronged.

Cain also took the decision to murder his brother because of the anger [Gen 4:8]. The only reasonable explanation for this behaviour is that in his anger Cain was led to do irrational things. There can be no justification for Cain channeling his anger on someone merely because the other person's offering had been accepted.

(4) How does sin operate? What does 'its desire is for you but you should rule over it' [Gen 4:7] mean?

When Cain was angry when his offering was not accepted, the LORD God talked to Cain about it. During this discussion some crucial information

The Old World

concerning how sin operates is revealed.

"If you do well, will you not be accepted? And if you do not do well, sin lies at the door. And its desire is for you, but you should rule over it." [Gen 4:7].

From this we understand the following:

- 'And if you do not do well, sin lies at the door': Starting on a clean slate, when our heart is perfect, sin does not have an entry point. In this scenario, only when we make an inappropriate choice sin has a possible entry point.
- 'Its desire is for you, but you should rule over it.': Sin when presented with an entry point, desires to consume a person. In this regard, sin is an 'active' entity. It is however required of human beings to rule over it or in other words to keep sin in check, despite all the active provocation from sin.

(5) Was Cain supposed to have been his brother's keeper [Gen 4:9]?

The LORD said to Cain, "Where is Abel your brother?". The very fact that the LORD asked this to Cain means that He expected Cain to have known or at least to care to know about the welfare of his brother.

(6) Because of Adam's disobedience the ground was cursed. Because of Cain's sin, he was cursed. How do these scenarios compare and contrast?

Adam's disobedience led the LORD God to curse the ground [Gen 3:17]. Adam now had to work harder to get his food. When Cain murdered Abel, the LORD cursed him and condemned him to be a fugitive and vagabond. He also declared that the earth will not yield its strength to Cain when he tills the ground [Gen 4:11-4:12].

In the case of Adam, when the ground was cursed at least Adam still had the faculties (like mind, will etc) to evaluate and respond appropriately to God. The hard work possibly can just keep him on his toes so that he may be alert to choose the right path at least going forward.

In the case of Cain, when he himself was cursed, it is very possible that the faculties required to evaluate and respond appropriately to God may be impaired enough to an extent his choices may progressively become worse. Please note that this only means a reduced possibility of getting back to God and not zero possibility.

VI. Spread Of Sin

(7) Could Cain have repented?

Given that God let Cain live even after he murdered Abel, Cain had the possibility of repenting and asking for forgiveness from God. Despite the fact that this is a possibility there doesn't seem to be an indication that he did repent.

(8) Cain said, "I shall be a fugitive and a vagabond on the earth, and it will be happen that anyone who finds me will kill me" [Gen 4:14]. Who can kill Cain?

Genesis 5:4 says Adam and Eve had sons and daughters apart from Cain, Abel and Seth. Any of these or their descendants are possible candidates to kill Cain.

(9) What was the mark on Cain?

We do not know what precisely was the mark on Cain. However what we do know is that that mark should be prominent enough for anyone who finds him to recognize that he has been 'marked' by God for protection [Gen 4:15].

B. Ungodly

(i) Bible Passage - Genesis 4:16-4:24

(ii) Summary

1. City [Gen 5:16-5:17]: Cain went out of the presence of the LORD and dwelt in the land of Nod on the east of Eden. Cain knew his wife and she conceived and bore Enoch. Cain then built a city and named the city after his son Enoch (Enoch means devotion).
2. Polygamy [Gen 5:18-5:19]: Lamech a descendant of Cain is the first person recorded to have had multiple wives.
3. Tent Dwellers [Gen 5:20]: Jabal, a son of Lamech seems to have introduced tent dwelling among humans.
4. Musical Instruments [Gen 5:21]: Jubal, another son of Lamech seems to have introduced musical instruments - the harp and the flute among humans.
5. Craftsmen in Bronze and Iron [Gen 5:22]: Tubal-Cain was an instructor of every craftsman in bronze and iron.
6. Murder [Gen 5:23-5:24]: Lamech ended up killing someone for wounding him.

The Old World

Meditation Notes
Entities

Questions

Exploration Areas

Cross References

Other Points

Reference Notes
(iii) Entities
The LORD, Cain, Enoch, Lamech, Jabal, Jubal, Tubal-Cain

(vi) Deeper Questions
(1) Was there the presence of God even outside Eden?
Genesis 4:16 tells us that Cain went out of the presence of the LORD when he was cursed and condemned to be a fugitive and a vagabond. This tells us that until this point in time he was in the presence of the LORD. What we do also know is that Cain was born outside the garden of Eden. The obvious conclusion is that the presence of the LORD (perhaps with a reduced intimacy) was there outside the garden of Eden also. The LORD's interaction with Cain in Genesis 4:4-4:15 is an example of Cain and Abel being in the presence of the LORD.

VI. Spread Of Sin

(2) Who did Cain marry?

Genesis 5:4 says Adam and Eve had sons and daughters apart from Cain, Abel and Seth. Cain would have married one of these daughters.

(3) Cain built a city and named it after his son, Enoch. What kind of city was this?

Cain was condemned to be a fugitive and vagabond when he murdered his brother Abel [Gen 4:11-4:12]. After experiencing a 'wandering' life he might have wanted to settle down for a bit somewhere. In this context it is interesting to see that Cain was the first recorded person to build a city [Gen 4:17]. Please note that this was called a city most likely not for the scale, but because of the existence of division of labour [Gen 4:20-4:22].

(4) Cain had named his son Enoch (Enoch means devotion). Why could this be?

It is possible Cain might have had a remote idea about devotion to God. This is possibly why he named his son Enoch. However there is no conclusive evidence to suggest that he did truly devote himself to God.

(5) Did Jubal played musical instruments for a living? Did Tubal-Cain instruct craftsmen in bronze and iron for a living?

The expression 'became the father of all those who dwell in tents and have livestock' [Gen 4:20] and the similar [Gen 4:21-4:22] seem to suggest that these were taken up as 'professions'.

(6) Were ancient civilizations primitive?

The first recorded city seems to have had a sophisticated division of labour [Gen 4:20-4:22]. This city was established by person who belonged to the second generation of human beings on planet earth, Cain. In other words the first established city was fairly close to the first man, Adam. This city had people who made a living out of playing music [Gen 4:21], people who were involved in using bronze and iron [Gen 4:22].

C. Godly

(i) Bible Passage - Genesis 4:25-5:32, 1 Ch 1:1-1:4

(ii) Summary

1. Seed [Gen 4:25, 5:1-5:3, 1 Ch 1:1]: Adam knew his wife again and bore a son Seth (Seth means 'appointed') named to emphasise that Eve had thought that God had appointed her another seed in the place of Abel. Seth was in the likeness of Adam and his image in the

The Old World

same way Adam was in the likeness of God.
2. Calling on the name of the LORD [Gen 4:26, 1 Ch 1:1]: When Enosh (Enosh means man or mankind) son of Seth was born, men began to call on the name of the LORD.
3. Dedication, judgment during death and walking with God [Gen 5:21-5:24, 1 Ch 1:3]: When Enoch, a descendant of Enosh begot Methuselah (Methuselah means 'man of the dart/spear', or alternatively 'his death shall bring judgment') he walked with God and he was not for God took him. Please note that Methuselah was the longest living person on the face of the earth.
4. Comfort [Gen 5:29, 1 Ch 1:3-1:4]: Lamech the son of Methuselah called his son Noah ('Noah' means 'comfort') saying 'This one will comfort us concerning our work and the toil of our hands, because of the ground which the LORD has cursed'.

Figure 8 - The Genealogy Of Adam

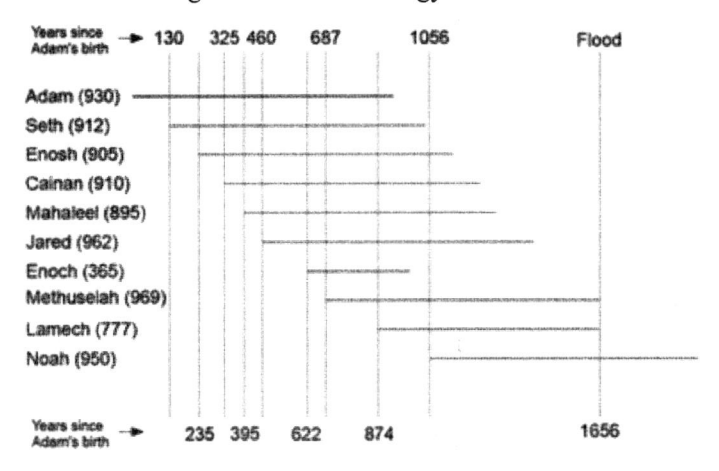

Years since Adam's birth →	130	325	460	687	1056	Flood
Adam (930)						
Seth (912)						
Enosh (905)						
Cainan (910)						
Mahaleel (895)						
Jared (962)						
Enoch (365)						
Methuselah (969)						
Lamech (777)						
Noah (950)						
Years since Adam's birth →	235	395	622	874		1656

Meditation Notes
Entities
....
....
....

VI. Spread Of Sin

Questions
....
....
....

Exploration Areas
....
....
....

Cross References
....
....
....

Other Points
....
....
....

Reference Notes

(iii) Entities

The LORD, Adam, Eve, Cain, Abel, Seth, Enosh, Enoch, Methuselah, Lamech, Noah.

(vi) Deeper Questions

(1) Could Eve have misunderstood the redemption plan?

Eve seems to have caught on to the idea of her 'seed' perhaps in anticipation of fulfilment of the promise in Genesis 3:15. When Abel was dead and Cain had become a fugitive, Eve seems to have been glad to have another 'seed' in Seth [Gen 4:25]. It is not quite clear if Eve expected the promise in Genesis 3:15 to happen perhaps during her life.

(2) Did Seth look like God?

It is very likely Seth looked like God [Gen 5:1, 5:3]. Please refer to the discussion II.A.vi.15.

(3) Why did men call on the name of the LORD after Enosh was born [Gen 4:26]?

The name 'Enosh' means 'man' or 'mankind'. It is possible that Seth named his son Enosh to emphasise that he was a mere 'man' pale in comparison

The Old World

before God. Perhaps it is this realisation that led people to call on the name of the LORD after Enosh was born.

(4) How many children did Adam and Eve have? Who did Cain marry? Was there incest in the first few generations of human existence and was it not bad?

Genesis 5:4 says Adam and Eve had sons and daughters apart from Cain, Abel and Seth. Cain or one of his brothers must have married one of their sisters. The rest may have married any unmarried woman in the family.

Incest in Adam's family would not have been an issue

1. Biological - close relatives marrying may produce genetic disorders in their children. This would not have been an issue in the second generation human beings as their genetic content would have been very rich and therefore not susceptible to genetic disorders
2. Legal - close relatives marrying was forbidden in the Bible during Mosaic time. However, Cain and his brothers lived about 2000 years before this.

(5) Why did Enoch begin to walk with God after he begot Methuselah [Gen 5:22]?

The name Methuselah means 'Man of the dart/spear', or alternatively 'his death shall bring judgment'. It is very possible that Enoch named his son Methuselah because God revealed to him there was going to come a judgment [Jude 14, 15] during the time of the death of his son. This is most likely the reason Enoch began walking with God after he begot Methuselah.

(6) Methuselah was the longest living man on the earth. Does this have any spiritual significance?

The name Methuselah means 'Man of the dart/spear', or alternatively 'his death shall bring judgment'. It is very likely God had revealed that there was going to come a judgment [Jude 14, 15] during the time of the death of Methuselah. In this context, Methuselah having the longest life on planet earth may show the long suffering that the LORD God goes through to delay destruction.

VI. Spread Of Sin

(7) What was Lamech seeking comfort from when he named Noah as 'comfort' ('Noah' means 'comfort)?

Lamech was seeking some sort of comfort concerning their work and the toil of our hands, because of the ground which the LORD had cursed [Gen 5:29]. In other words, Lamech expected Noah to somehow usher in a time of easier access to food.

(8) Could Lamech have met Adam?

Please refer to figure 2. It is interesting to note that all in the patriarchal line of Noah up to and including Lamech would have lived contemporary to all their forefathers going up to Adam. It is very likely also that they would have met each other in person and have shared their experiences with each other. In other words, everyone up to Lamech in this line could have got to know about Adam's experience first hand. Noah on the other hand was contemporary to Methuselah. If Methuselah knew about the judgment as discussed for questions 5 and 6, he could have very well discussed about these things with Noah.

(vii) Explore

(1) Extra-Biblical Evidence For Long Age:

There is one more document on top of the Biblical account in Genesis 4:25-5:32 that mentions about ages of people that correspond to this period. This is the Sumerian King List. The Sumerian King List, interestingly gives ages for kings prior to a 'notable' flood at several magnitude higher than the ages of the kings after the flood just like the Bible.

In his article, "The Antediluvian Patriarchs And The Sumerian King List", dated 1st of Dec 1998, Raúl López studies the merit of this document and observes that the Sumerian King List has a striking parallel to the account in Genesis 4:25-5:32.

The Old World

Figure/Extract 9 - Sumerian King List

*"After the kingship descended from heaven, the kingship was in Eridu.
In Eridu, Alulim became king; he ruled for 28,800 years.
Alalgar ruled for 36,000 years.
Two kings; they ruled for 64800 years.
Then Eridu fell and the kingship was taken to Bad-tibira.
In Bad-tibira, Enmen-lu-ana ruled for 43,200 years.
Enmen-gal-ana ruled for 28,800 years.
The divine Dumuzi, the shepherd, ruled for 36,000 years.
Three kings; they ruled for 108,000 years.
Then Bad-tibira fell and the kingship was taken to Larak.
In Larak, En-sipad-zid-ana ruled for 28,800 years.
One king; he ruled for 28,800 years.
Then Larak fell and the kingship was taken to Sippar.
In Sippar, Enmen-dur-ana became king; he ruled for 21,000 years.
One king; he ruled for 21000 years.
Then Sippar fell and the kingship was taken to Šuruppak.
In Šuruppak, Ubara-Tutu became king; he ruled for 18,600 years.
One king; he ruled for 18,600 years.
Five cities; eight kings ruled for 385,200 years.
Then the Flood swept over.
After the Flood had swept over, and the kingship had descended from heaven, the kingship was in Kiš.
In Kiš, Gišur became king; he ruled for 1,200 years.
Kullassina-bel ruled for 900 years.
Nan-GIŠ-lišma ruled for 1,200 years."*

VII
Pause & Consider - How Would The World Have Looked Like With Cain's Line And Seth's Line Inhabiting The Earth?

After Cain had murdered Abel, he had left his parents to be a vagabond. The Bible doesn't clarify when Cain got married, but it does clarify that he had children even while he was a vagabond. In the meantime Seth is most likely to have led a settled life, perhaps closer to his parents.

Cain's lineage went onto at least up to seven generations including Cain. Seth's lineage went onto nine generations including Seth. It is not quite clear if these two lineages ever crossed paths again.

In Cain's lineage there are explicit records about conflict, murder, polygamy etc. There is not much information available about Seth's family for us to see if every one of them in that lineage were Godly. However, there is explicit records to suggest that at least some of them like Enoch, Noah were Godly.

Please also note that Adam and Eve had other children. We do not have enough information from scriptures to see how their behaviour was.

Figure/Table 10 - The Godly And The Ungodly Lines

Generation No	Person in Cain's Line	Person in Seth's Line
1	Cain	Seth
2	Enoch	Enosh
3	Irad	Cainan
4	Mehujael	Mahalalel
5	Methushael	Jared
6	Lamech	Enoch
7	Jabal and Jubal (Through Adah), Tubal Cain and Naamah (Through Zillah)	Methuselah
8		Lamech
9		Noah

The Old World

VIII
Judgment (Noahic Flood)

"...when once the Divine longsuffering waited in the days of Noah, while the ark was being prepared, in which a few, that is, eight souls, were saved through water."
1 Peter 3:20

A. State of the World

(i) Bible Passage - Genesis 6:1-6:12

(ii) Summary

1. Marriages & Nephilims [Gen 6:1-6:2, 6:4]: Men multiplied on the face of the earth and daughters were were born to them. Sons of God saw the daughters of men, that they were beautiful and they took wives for themselves of all whom they chose. The product of sons of God and daughters of men were giants and they were mighty men and men of renown.

2. The LORD's decision to not strive [Gen 6:3]: The LORD was not happy and He decided that His Spirit will not strive with man forever because he was just flesh. He also determined that men's days shall be 120 years.

3. Further degeneration - wickedness of man [Gen 6:5, 6:11-6:12]: The wickedness of man was great on earth, and every intent of the thoughts of his heart was only evil continually.

4. The LORD's decision to destroy because of man's evil inclinations [Gen 6:6-6:7]: The LORD was sorry that he had made man on the earth and was grieved in his heart. The LORD decided to destroy man (along with beasts, creeping things and birds of the air) from the face of the earth.

5. Noah's testimony [Gen 6:8-6:10]: Noah found grace in the eyes of the LORD. Noah was a just man, perfect (blameless) in his generations. Noah walked with God.

6. Further degeneration - corruption of all flesh and violence [Gen 6:11-6:12]: God looked upon the earth to double check and then confirmed that it was indeed corrupt. All flesh had corrupted their way on the earth and the earth was filled with their violence.

The Old World

7. The LORD's decision to destroy because of all flesh [Gen 6:13]: God decided that it was time for the end of all flesh.

Meditation Notes

Entities

....
....
....

Questions

....
....
....

Exploration Areas

....
....
....

Cross References

....
....
....

Other Points

....
....
....

Reference Notes

(iii) Entities

The LORD, sons of God, daughters of men, giants aka Nephilims, Noah, Shem, Ham and Japheth

(vi) Deeper Questions

(1) Who are referred to as the sons of God [Gen 6:2]?

The sons of God referred to in Genesis 6:2 are most likely angels. Through the fact that these angels are doing things which are displeasing to the LORD it can be understood that these are the fallen angels.

(2) "My Spirit shall not strive with man forever, for he is indeed flesh" [Gen 6:3]. Why did the LORD come to this decision?

VIII. Judgment (Noahic Flood)

The summary of activities given for the specific period referred to in Genesis 6:1 is that the sons of God took wives for themselves from the daughters of men. In other words, it seems like the primary motive of people during this time was to give and take in marriage. This of course would have come at the cost of having God and worship to Him as the primary motive of human existence. This is what led the LORD to the conclusion that he would not strive with man forever.

(3) "Yet his days days shall be one hundred and twenty years". Who do this 120 years apply to?

It is possible that the 120 years applied to the time between the LORD's decision and the time at which he would eventually destroy the world through the flood. However, the decision, 'My Spirit shall not strive with man forever' seems to indicate that the decision was in regards to any man as opposed to men of those times. In other words, it seems like the LORD was determining to reduce the lifespan of human beings to something around 120 years.

(4) "Those were the mighty men who were of old, men of renown" [Gen 6:4]. If these were men of renown why was the LORD not glad with this situation?

These mighty men were only men of renown among the other men on the earth. What pleases man does not necessarily please God. The LORD seemed to care less of the fact that men were mighty.

(5) Initially the LORD decided not to just strive with humans [Gen 6:3]. Subsequently he decided to destroy humans (along with beasts, creeping things and birds) because of his evil inclinations [Gen 6:7]. However he waited until the earth was filled with corruption and violence because all flesh to destroy the world [Gen 6:13]. Why was this?

The LORD seems to have been extremely patient even with the people during Noah's time. He initially withheld destruction soon after people's concentration turned purely to giving and taking in marriage [Gen 6:3]. Even after realising that man's thoughts were evil continually, he did not seem to have brought destruction immediately [Gen 6:7]. It was only when the earth was filled with violence and was corrupt both because of all flesh [Gen 6:12-6:13] the LORD ultimately brought destruction. This demonstrates the fact that the LORD suffers long for man because of his love.

(6) "Noah found grace in the eyes of the LORD" [Gen 6:8]. Was there no

The Old World

one apart from Noah who found grace in the eyes of the LORD during this time? How about Methuselah?

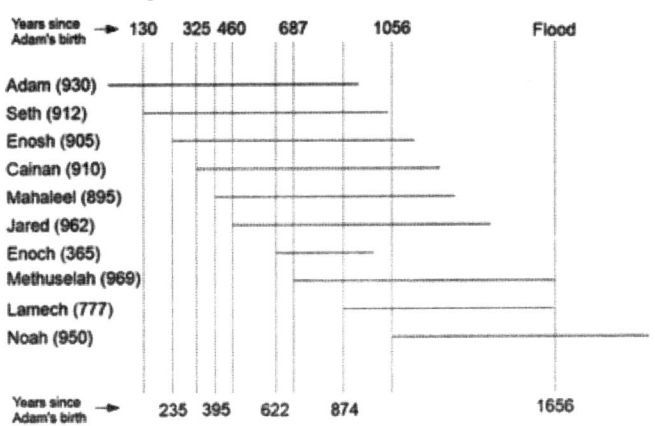

Figure 11 - The Timing Of The Flood

Years since Adam's birth →	130	325	460	687	1056	Flood
Adam (930)						
Seth (912)						
Enosh (905)						
Cainan (910)						
Mahaleel (895)						
Jared (962)						
Enoch (365)						
Methuselah (969)						
Lamech (777)						
Noah (950)						
Years since Adam's birth →	235	395	622	874		1656

Please note that by the time the LORD ultimately brought about the flood all the forefathers of Noah (along the paternal line) had passed away. It was Methuselah who would have been the last to die and that too just before the flood.

(7) Grace is unmerited favour. If Noah was a just man, perfect in his generations [Gen 6:9], why does he need unmerited favour from God [Gen 6:8]?

There is no indication that Noah was a sinless person. The term 'perfect' can imply someone who is blameless i.e. someone who had sinned but the sin had been dealt with through appropriate repentance and forgiveness. If this were the case with Noah he would still be someone who depended on the grace of God to be preserved from destruction of the wicked.

(8) "The earth also was corrupt before God, and the earth was filled with violence. So God looked upon the earth, and indeed it was corrupt; for all flesh had corrupted their way on the earth" [Gen 6:11-6:12]. Explain.

During creation, every animal seemingly was docile [Gen 2:19-2:20] and man was obedient to God. By the time of Noah this seems to have changed a lot to an extent every thought of man was evaluated to be evil [Gen 6:5]. Somehow man's attitude seems to have trickled down into the attitude of the beasts of the earth also [Gen 6:7]. Ultimately, all flesh have turned to

VIII. Judgment (Noahic Flood)

violent ways [Gen 6:11], perhaps to show anger, selfishness etc. It is possible that man showed this corruption by reckless violence and murder, whereas animals showed this corruption by moving far away from their original docile attitude to even have other animals killed.

(vii) Explore

(1) Evidence For Giants and Violence From Different Cultures:
In various Indo-European mythologies, gigantic peoples are featured as primeval creatures associated with chaos and the wild nature, and they are frequently portrayed to be in conflict with the gods, be they Olympian, Celtic, Hindu or Norse. Giants also often play similar roles in the mythologies and folklore of other, non Indo-European peoples, such as in the Nartian traditions. These traditions bear a great degree of overlap with the Biblical account in Genesis 6:1-6:12.

B. Preparation for the Flood
(i) Bible Passage - Genesis 6:13-7:9
(ii) Summary
1. Judgment [Gen 6:13]: God communicated to Noah that He had determined the end of all flesh because the earth was filled with violence. God was going to destroy the earth with them.
2. Instruction about the ark [Gen 6:14-6:16]: The following are the specification of the ark which God wanted Noah to build.
   a. Ark is to be made of gopherwood with rooms and covered both inside and outside using pitch.
   b. Dimensions of the ark - 300 Cubits (length) x 50 cubits (width) x 30 cubits (height). 1 Cubit = 1' 6" (1.5 Feet) minimum.
   c. Number of decks: 3.
   d. A window for the ark a cubit from above.
   e. A door for the ark on the side.
3. Flood foretold [Gen 6:17]: God was going to send flood waters on the earth to destroy from under heaven all flesh in which is the breath of life and everything on the earth shall die.
4. Promised covenant [Gen 6:18]: God intended to establish his covenant with Noah,ah, his sons, his wife and his son's wives shall go into the ark.
5. Instruction about animals [Gen 6:19-6:20]: Noah shall bring 2 (a male and a female) of every kind of all flesh into the ark, of birds,

The Old World

animals and creeping things.
6. Food [Gen 6:21]: Noah is to take of all food that is eaten as food for himself, his household and all the animals with him in the ark.
7. Noah's obedience [Gen 6:22]: Noah did according to all that God commanded him.
8. Entering into the ark [Gen 7:1]: The LORD asked Noah to get into the ark, he and his household because he was found righteous before God in that generation.
9. Updated instruction about animals [Gen 7:2-7:3]: Noah is to take with him seven pairs (a male and a female) of every clean animal, a pair (a male and a female) of every unclean animal, and seven pairs (a male and a female) of birds of the air.
10. Rain foretold [Gen 7:4]: Seven days after God asking Noah and his family to enter the ark (along with the animals), the LORD was going to send rain on the earth forty days and forty nights and will destroy from the face of the earth all living things that God had made.
11. Noah's continued obedience [Gen 7:5]: Noah did according to all that the LORD commanded him.
12. Animals' entry into the ark [Gen 7:8-7:9]: All clean beasts, unclean beasts, of everything that creeps, two by two they went into the ark to Noah.

Meditation Notes

Entities

....
....
....

Questions

....
....
....

Exploration Areas

....
....
....

VIII. Judgment (Noahic Flood)

Cross References

....
....
....

Other Points

....
....
....

Reference Notes

(iii) Entities

The LORD, Noah, his wife, his three sons and their wives.

(vi) Deeper Questions

(1) "And behold, I will destroy them with the earth" [Gen 6:13]. What is the implication of 'with the earth'?

God had decided that he was going to destroy the whole world because of progressive degeneration. It is important to note that by the time the LORD decided to destroy the world, He had judged that the earth was corrupt and was filled with violence. Because of this the LORD intended to destroy even the earth. In other words the postdiluvian earth could be markedly different from the antediluvian earth to an extent the latter could be referred to have been destroyed. Please also note that this destruction of the earth could also have a say in the reduction in general human lifespan (Refer to VIII.A.vi.3).

(2) What entities were the flood intended to destroy?

The flood was intended to destroy all flesh i.e. birds, land animals (including the creeping animals) and man. Please note that he did not intend to destroy sea creatures and vegetation of all sorts.

(3) What is Gopherwood [Gen 6:14]?

It is not precisely known what Gopherwood is.

(4) Was the ark big enough to carry all the animals and birds God wanted it to carry?

It is understood that the 'kinds' of animals and birds that Noah had to take into the ark correspond to 'families' as per modern taxonomy. Furthermore, Noah was not required to take in fully grown specimens and even the young ones of huge animals are generally relatively manageable in size.

The Old World

All these animals according to the number specified by God could have been easily accommodated in 45,000 square cubits of floor space in the 3 tier ark.

Figure/Table 12 - Animals And Birds In Noah's Ark

Type	Num of Genera (based on "Noah's Ark: A Feasibility Study by John Woodmorappe")	Number of Families (The 'Ark Encounter' project led by 'Answers in Genesis')	Number of Species
Mammals	3,714	239	5,500
Birds	2,301	299	10,500
Reptiles	1,862	321	10,000
Amphibians	Not available	70	7,000
Sea Animals	Not in the ark		230,000
Arthropods	Possibly in the ark but insignificant in total area occupied		1,100,000
Total	7,877	938	1,363,000

Courtesy: Answers in Genesis.

Figure 13 - Comparing Noah's Ark With Modern Ships

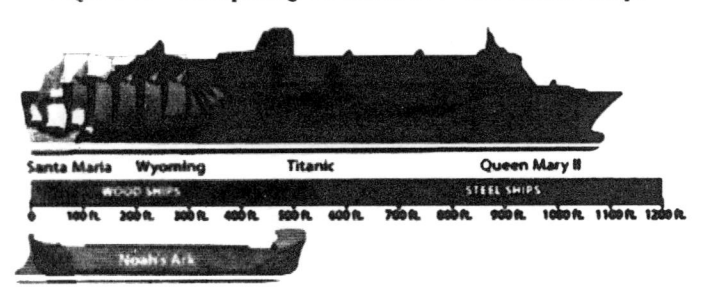

Courtesy: Answers in Genesis

VIII. Judgment (Noahic Flood)

(5) How many animals of each kind did God ask Noah to take with him into the ark? Two [Gen 6:19-6:20] or seven pairs [Gen 7:2-7:3]?

Noah had to take in seven pairs of clean animals and one pair of unclean animals. He was also required to take seven pairs of birds. It is commonly understood that God's initial instruction was only in respect to keeping species alive whereas His subsequent instruction also includes the possible burnt offerings after the flood. It is important to note that these are not contradictory but complementary instructions.

(6) What was going to happen to plants and sea creatures?

No specific information is available regarding plants and sea creatures. It is not hard to imagine that at least some of the sea creatures would have survived a flood. I am not aware of any study done to evaluate how plants behave during floods similar to Noahic flood.

C. The Flood

(i) Bible Passage - Genesis 7:10-8:19

(ii) Summary

1. Time [Gen 7:6, 7:11]: In the six hundredth year of Noah's life, in the second month, the seventeenth day of the month.
2. Source of the water [Gen 7:11-7:12]:
    a. Fountains of the great deep were broken up
    b. Windows of heaven were opened
    c. Rain on earth for forty days and forty nights
3. Entering the ark [Gen 7:13-7:16]: Noah and his sons Shem, Ham and Japheth and Noah's wife and the three wives of his sons entered the ark - they and every beast after its kind, all cattle after their kind, every creeping thing that creeps on the earth after its kind, and every bird after its kind, every bird of every sort. They went in two by two, male and female of all flesh, went in as God had commanded Noah and the LORD shut him in.
4. Flood and destruction [Gen 7:17-7:24]:
    a. Flood was there for 40 days.
    b. Waters prevailed 15 cubits from the top of the mountains.
    c. All flesh died that moved on the earth - birds, cattle, creeping thing and man. All in whose nostrils was the

The Old World

        breath of the spirit of life, all that was on the dry land, died.
- d. The waters prevailed on the earth 150 days.
5. The recession of the flood [Gen 8:1-8:5]:
    a. God remembered Noah and made a wind to pass over the earth and waters subsided.
    b. All the sources of water were stopped - the fountains of the deep and the windows of heaven were stopped. Rain from heaven was restrained.
    c. The ark rested in seventh month, the seventeenth day of the month on the mountains of Ararat.
    d. In the tenth month, on the first day of the month, the tops of the mountains were seen.
6. The birds tests and the final observation [Gen 8:6-8:14]:
    a. Raven test: At the end of forty days, Noah opened the window of the ark which he had made. The raven kept going to and fro until the waters had dried up from the earth.
    b. Dove test: Noah sent a dove out but the dove found no resting place for the sole of her foot, and she returned into the ark into him for the waters were on the face of the whole earth. The dove returned into the ark. Noah sent it again after seven days. Then the dove came to him in the evening with a freshly plucked olive leaf indicating that the waters had abated. Noah sent it again after seven days and the dove did not return again to him.
    c. In Noah's six hundred and first year, in the first month, the first day of the month, that the waters were dried up from the earth. Noah removed the covering of the ark and looked and indeed the surface of the ground was dry.
    d. In the second month, on the twenty seventh day of the month, the earth was dried.
7. Repopulation of the earth [Gen 8:15-8:19]: God asked Noah to go out of the ark, him and his household and all the beasts, creeping things and birds. God asked them to abound on the earth and be fruitful and multiply.

VIII. Judgment (Noahic Flood)

Meditation Notes
Entities
....
....
....

Questions
....
....
....

Exploration Areas
....
....
....

Cross References
....
....
....

Other Points
....
....
....

Reference Notes
(iii) Entities
The LORD, Noah, his wife, his three sons and their wives, Mount Ararat.
(vi) Deeper Questions
(1) "All the fountains of the great deep were broken up and the windows of heaven were opened. And the rain was on the earth forty days and forty nights" [Gen 7:11-7:12]. Where are the fountains of the great deep and windows of heaven today?
The LORD had intended to destroy all flesh along with the earth [Gen 6:13]. In other words, the features on the earth today may not be representative of the features on the earth before the flood. There seems to be two prominent sources of flood water which are no longer present in the same form - namely, windows of heaven and fountains of the great deep.

The Old World

(2) How high did the waters fill the earth? Was 15 cubits of waters able to submerge all of the mountains?

It is understood that the expression 'the waters prevailed fifteen cubits upward' indicates that the waters prevailed up and above the tallest mountains by about 15 cubits. It is however important to understand that the mountains of that time may not be the same or similar as of the mountains of today. The Noahic flood would have had cataclysmic impact such that many new mountain ranges might have formed as a result of the flood and many old mountain ranges might have been destroyed.

(3) *"The ark rested in the seventh month, the seventeenth day of the month on the mountains of Ararat" [Gen 8:4]. "In the tenth month on the first day of the month the tops of the mountains were seen" [Gen 8:5]. Are these not contradictory statements?*

No. These are not contradictory statements. The ark, of course would have a portion submerged under water. It is with this submerged portion that it would have rested on the mountains of Ararat. When the ark rested for the first time, the mountains of Ararat might have still been submerged in water.

(4) Was the Noahic flood a world wide flood or local flood?

The LORD intended to destroy all the flesh along with the earth [Gen 6:13]. The Bible says the flood covered all the high hills under the whole heaven [Gen 7:19]. In other words, this was a worldwide flood. This flood happened about 1650 years after creation of Adam. Noah belonged to the tenth generation from Adam. A conservative estimate for the human population on earth at the time of the flood would be many millions. These several millions would have lived across a wide area of the earth's landmass. Add to this the multitude of animals and the fact that the LORD wanted to destroy the earth also. It is therefore understandable to see why the LORD sent a world wide flood.

VIII. Judgment (Noahic Flood)

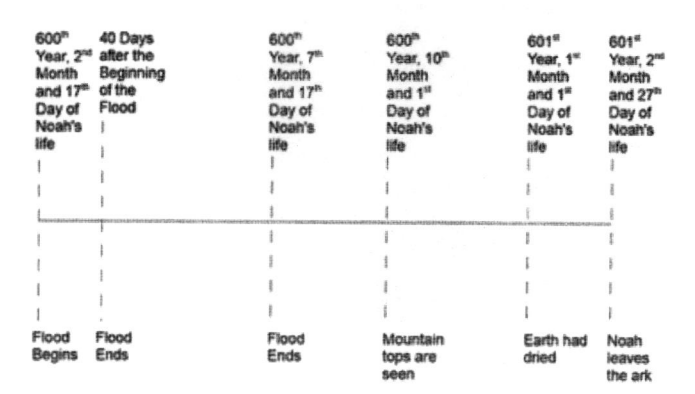

Figure 14 - Noahic Flood - Timeline

600th Year, 2nd Month and 17th Day of Noah's life	40 Days after the Beginning of the Flood	600th Year, 7th Month and 17th Day of Noah's life	600th Year, 10th Month and 1st Day of Noah's life	601st Year, 1st Month and 1st Day of Noah's life	601st Year, 2nd Month and 27th Day of Noah's life
Flood Begins	Flood Ends	Flood Ends	Mountain tops are seen	Earth had dried	Noah leaves the ark

(vii) Explore

(1) Extra-Biblical Evidences For Noahic Flood:

(a) Flood traditions

Epic of Gilgamesh: There are archaeological artefacts (dating from about 2100 BC) for a story that dates back to the Akkadian period, that talk about Gilgamesh, a legendary ruler of Uruk meeting Utnapishtim. Utnapishtim closely resembles Biblical Noah in that he was forewarned of a plan by the gods to send a great flood. He built a boat and loaded it with all his precious possessions, his kith and kin, domesticated and wild animals and skilled craftsmen of every kind. Utnapishtim survived the flood for six days while mankind was destroyed, before landing on a mountain called Nimush. He released a dove and a swallow but they did not find dry land to rest on, and returned. Finally a raven that he released did not return, showing that the waters must have receded.

The Old World

Figure 15 - Gilgamesh Epic

"GilgameshTablet". Licensed under Public Domain via Wikimedia Commons - http://commons.wikimedia.org/wiki/File:GilgameshTablet.jpg#/media/File:Gilgamesh Tablet.jpg

Atrahasis Epic: Dating to 17th Century BC, Atrahasis epic portrays Atrahasis who closely resembles Biblical Noah. Enlil, the god of Earth plans to destroy humans with plague, famine, drought and finally a flood. However, each time Enki, the god of subterranean sweet water instructs one of the humans, Atrahasis, to survive the disasters. The god gives Atrahasis seven days warning of the flood, and he builds a boat, loads it with his possessions, animals and birds. He is subsequently saved while the rest of humankind is destroyed.

Figure 16 - Atrahasis Epic

"Bm-epic-g". Licensed under Public Domain via Wikimedia Commons - http://commons.wikimedia.org/wiki/File:Bm-epic-g.jpg#/media/File:Bm-epic-g.jpg

VIII. Judgment (Noahic Flood)

Chinese Pictogram For Boat:

The Chinese language pictogram for the word boat is literally just the pictograms of 'vessel', 'eight' and 'mouth'/'men' put together.

Figure 17 - Boat In Chinese

船 (boat) = 舟 (vessel) + 八 (eight) + 口 (mouth)

Courtesy: http://bibleprobe.com/chinese.htm

(b) Geology

Dr. Andrew Snelling in his article 'What are some of the best flood evidences' written on Feb 13 2015, gives the following geologic evidences for a world wide flood consistent with the narration in Genesis 7:10-8:19.

1. Fossils of sea creatures found high above sea level due to ocean waters having flooded over the continents: For instance Kaibab limestone in Grand Canyon has marine fossils about 7,000 - 8,000 feet above the sea level. This limestone was therefore deposited beneath lime sediment-charged ocean waters, which swept over northern Arizona (and beyond).

2. Rapid burial of plants and animals across the world: Countless billions of plant and animal fossils are found in extensive "graveyards" where they had to be buried rapidly on a massive scale. Often the fine details of the creatures are exquisitely preserved. This testifies to the rapid burial of plants and animals on a global scale in a watery cataclysm and its immediate aftermath.

3. Rapidly deposited sediment layers spread across vast areas: Sediment layers that spread across vast continents are evidence that water covered the continents in the past. Even more dramatic are the fossil-bearing sediment layers that were deposited rapidly right across many or most of the continents at the same time. To catastrophically deposit such extensive sediment layers implies global flooding of the continents.

The Old World

4. Sediments transported long distances: The Coconino Sandstone, seen spectacularly in the walls of the Grand Canyon, has an average thickness of 315 feet, covers an area of at least 200,000 square miles, and thus contains at least 10,000 cubic miles of sand. Where did this sand come from and how do we know? The only logical and viable explanation is the global cataclysmic Genesis Flood. Only the water currents of a global ocean, lasting a few months, could have transported such huge volumes of sediments right across North America to deposit the thick strata sequences which blanket the continent.

5. Rapid or no erosion between strata: The fossil-bearing portion of the geologic record consists of tens of thousands of feet of sedimentary layers, of which about 4,500 feet are exposed in the walls of the Grand Canyon. If this enormous thickness of sediments were deposited over 500 or more million years, then some boundaries between layers should show evidence of millions of years of slow erosion, just as erosion is occurring on some land surfaces today. On the other hand, if this enormous thickness of sediments were all deposited in just over a year during the global cataclysmic Genesis Flood, then the boundaries between the layers should show evidence of continuous rapid deposition, with only occasional evidence of rapid erosion, or of no erosion at all. And that's exactly what we find, as illustrated by strata boundaries in the Grand Canyon.

6. Many strata laid down in rapid succession: When solid, hard rock is bent (or folded) it invariably fractures and breaks because it is brittle. Rock will bend only if it is still soft and pliable—"plastic" like modeling clay or children's play-dough. It's possible to see these folded sedimentary layers in several side canyons. For example, the folded Tapeats Sandstone can be seen in Carbon Canyon. Notice that these sandstone layers were bent 90° (a right angle), yet the rock was not fractured or broken in the fold axis or hinge line (apex) of the fold. Similarly, the folded Muav and Redwall Limestone layers can be seen along nearby Kwagunt Creek. The folding of these limestones did not cause them to

VIII. Judgment (Noahic Flood)

fracture and break either, as would be expected for ancient, brittle rocks. The obvious conclusion is that these sandstone and limestone layers were all folded and bent while the sediments were still soft and pliable, and very soon after they were deposited.

The Old World

IX
Pause & Consider - What Are The Implications Of Noahic Flood?

(1) Implications Of Noahic flood

Noahic flood, as per the details available in the Bible, was a worldwide catastrophe. God's intention was that, through the flood, He would destroy not alone all life (life outside), but also the earth [Gen 6:13]. The idea of this catastrophe is also affirmed through different extra-Biblical sources as discussed in VIII.C.vii.1.

There are multiple implications of Noahic flood. The common theme across these multiple implications is that what we know as the world today may not be representative of the world in the past.

(a) Assumptions In Examining Artefacts:

There are at least two possible windows for exploring the state of the earth before the flood viz. paleontological and geological records. However, because we have evidence for a worldwide catastrophic flood both from the Bible and other archaeological artefacts, when we examine paleontological and geological artefacts, we must accommodate for catastrophic events.

However, it is popular among many people to completely ignore this and assert a relatively stable earth ('uniformitarianism'), which at best leads to inaccurate evaluation of the artefacts and at worst indicates a deliberate unscientific and irrational precommitment to excluding God. This is the main problem with several 'dating' exercises. Fossils are dated to millions of years in the past, using 'uniformitarianism' as an assumption, and then that same 'evidence' is used to disprove the Bible. This is a clear example of circular reasoning.

(b) Geography:

Many prominent geographical features such as the tall Himalayas, continental and polar ice sheets and alpine glaciers should be interpreted with Noahic flood in mind. For instance, the continental and polar ice sheets and the alpine glaciers, were most likely formed during the rapid fluctuation in the weather during Noahic flood. Similarly, Himalayas and the other tall mountain ranges were possibly formed for the first time due to

The Old World

massive upheaval of the earth during Noahic flood.

(c) Geology:

Many, when studying geologic records, normally assume 'uniformitarianism' to be true not leaving any place for a catastrophe. With this as the basis, they would anticipate things like Grand Canyon etc to have formed over millions of years. On top of this, when dating many fossils based on ages attributed to different layers of the rocks, they necessarily force the age of the fossils to comply with the assumption of uniformitarianism. This mindset ought to be revised. Layers of rocks in places like Grand Canyon ought to be seen as layers laid down in rapid succession perhaps within the same day or across few days.

(2) The Old World

Alfred M. Rehwinkel, who was both a theologian and geologist, in his work 'The Flood' makes a couple of observations about the world before the flood.

(a) Vegetation And People:

Fossils of plants and man-made implements found in the Sahara show that this great African desert was at one time covered in luxuriant vegetation and was inhabited by man.

(b) Uniformly Mild Climate:

Fossils show that there was a uniformly mild climate in high and low altitudes of both the northern and the southern hemisphere. That is, there was a perfectly uniform, non-zonal, mild, and spring like climate in every part of the globe.

(c) Coal Beds:

An irrefutable proof for the unparalleled luxuriance of plant life in that pre-historic world is the great coal beds found in every continent of the earth today.

X
Glossary

120 years	81
Abel	20, 67, 73
Acquired	67
Adah	79
Adam	20, 40, 51, 65, 67, 73
Adam and Eve seal	61
Akkadian	61, 93
Alfred M. Rehwinkel	100
Alpine glaciers	99
Ancient civilizations	38, 73
Andrew Snelling	38, 95
Animals	20, 33, 85
Angry	67
Answers in Genesis	39, 59, 88
Ararat	90
Ark	85
Arthropods	88
Assyria	40
Atrahasis	94
Bacterium	33
Bdellium	40
Beast of the field	40
Beasts of the land	15
Beginning	15
Belly	56
Biblical creationism	24, 34
Big bang model	20
Biological	31, 76
Birds	15, 81

Birth	46, 62
Black holes	23
Blood	67
Boat	94, 95
Breath	39, 43, 67
Bronze	71
Brother's keeper	67
Cain	20, 60, 67, 79
Cainan	79
Carbon canyon	96
Cataclysm	95
Cherubim	62
Christian Apologetics and Research Ministry	39
Christoph Zollikofer	32
Celtic	85
Chinese	95
City	71
Clean animals	89
CMB (Cosmic Microwave Background) radiation	22
Coal beds	100
Coelacanths	38
Comfort	74
Commandment	40, 50, 51, 65
Conception	56
Corrupt	81
Cosmological models	24
Craftsmen	71
Creation Ministries International	39
Creeping things	16
Cultures	62
Curse	

Ground	57
Cain	67
Cush	41
Darkness	15
Dart	74
Darwinian evolution	20
David Lordkipanidze	32
Day-Age (creationism)	25
Daughters of men	81
Disobedience	51
Distant starlight	28
Dissimilarities	31
Division of labour	73
Death	21, 57, 66, 69, 74, 76
Deceived	56
Design	32
Destroy	81
Disobeyed	87
DNA	31
Door	67
Dove	90
Dust	23, 24, 39, 56
Earth	15
Eden	39
Edwin Hubble	23
Elohim	16
Emmanuel	47
Employment	64
Enki	94
Enlil	94
Enmity	56
Enoch	

Cain's line	71, 79
Seth's line	74, 79
Enosh	74, 79
Epic of Gilgamesh	93
Eve	46, 57
Evening and morning	19
Explanatory power	27, 38
Euphrates	40
Fear	52
Fertility	62
Fig leaves	51
Firmament	15
Firstling	67
Flagellum	32
Flaming sword	58
Flesh	82
Flock	67
Flute	71
Fossils	33, 37, 38, 95
Fountains	89
Fruit	21, 44
Fugitive	67
Galaxies	22
Gap (creationism)	25
Geography	99
Geology	95, 100
Geological	99
Georgian national museum	32
Giants	81
Gihon	41
Gilgamesh	93

God	15
Good	21
Gopherwood	85
Grace	81
Gradual change	20
Grand Canyon	33, 95
Graveyards	95
Great deep	89
Guard	62
Ham	82, 89
Harp	71
Havilah	40
Heavens	15, 89
Helper	40
Herb of the field	39
Herbs	16
Hiddekel	40
Himalayas	99
Historical validity	27, 36
Holiness	64
Ice sheets	99
Image	
Adam	15
Seth	73
Index fossils	37
Indo-European	85
Irad	79
Irrational	69
Iron	71
Irreducible complexity	33
Incest	76

Jabal	71, 79
Japheth	82, 89
Jared	79
John Woodmorappe	88
Jubal	71, 79
Judgment	55, 74
Kaibab limestone	38, 95
Kill	61, 68
Kinds	31, 87
Kingdoms of Biology	30
Kwagunt creek	96
Lamech	
Cain's line	71, 79
Seth's line	74, 79
Legal	76
Light	15
Lights	15
Limestones	96
Living fossil	38
Livestock	73
Long age	77
LORD God	39
Mahalel	79
Mammals	88
Man	74
Man of dart/spear	74
Marine fossil	95
Mark	67
Marriages	81
Marry	73, 76
Mechanism	67

Mehujael	79
Methuselah	74, 79
Methushael	79
Mighty men	81
Moral compass	50, 65
Muav	96
Multilayer fossil	38
Multiverse	22
Murder	67, 71, 79
Musical instruments	71
Mythological	62
Mythologies	85
Naamah	79
Naked	40, 46, 51
Nartian	85
Nephilims	81
Nimush	93
Noah	74, 79, 81
Noahic flood	81, 99
Nod	71
Norse	85
Objective boundary	31
Olympian	85
Onyx	41
Pain	56
Paleontological	99
Perfection	64
Philosophical validity	26, 36
Pishon	40
Plastic	96
Polygamy	71, 79

Professions	67
Progressive creationism	35
Provisions	39
Punctuations	31
Punishment	68
Rain	39, 86
Raúl López	77
Raven	90
Redshift	22, 23
Redwall limestone	96
Regeneration	62
Relational	42, 65
Reproduction	31, 46, 66
Reptiles	88
Rest	16
Rib	40
Sabbath day	16
Sacrifice	61
Science (journal)	32
Seas	15
Sea creatures/animals	15, 87
Sedimentary rocks	33
Sediments	37, 96
Seed	21, 56, 73
Serpent	51, 56
Seth	73, 79
Sevenfold	68
Sexual reproduction	31, 66
Shem	82, 89
Similarities	31
Sin	46, 60

Skull	32
Sons of God	82
Sorry	81
Spear	67, 74
Species	28, 31, 88
Spirit	15, 81
Spirit of God	15
Steady state (naturalism)	25
Strata	96
Strive	81
Sumerian king list	78
Sweat	57
Tapeats sandstone	96
Taxonomy	21
Tbilisi	32
Tent	71
Theistic evolution	35
Thistles	50, 57
Thorns	50, 57
Tigris	40
Toil	57, 74
Tree of knowledge of good and evil	41, 52
Tree of life	41, 58
Trees	15
Tubal-Cain	71, 79
Tunic	57
Umbilical cord	62
Unanswered questions	27, 39
Unclean animals	86
Uniform CMB temperature	23
Uniformitarianism	34, 99

Universe	22
University of Zurich	32
Ur	61
Uruk	93
Utnapishtim	93
Variety of life	28
Vagabond	67
Voice	58, 67
Waters	15, 85
Windows	89
Woman	18, 40
Work	16, 62
Yom	19, 41
Zillah	79